DAVID BELLAMY

WILDERNESS ARTIST

DAVID BELLAMY
WILDERNESS ARTIST

HarperCollins*Publishers*

To the memory of my grandfather, James Samuel Bellamy, from whom I inherited my great love of the wild country.

ACKNOWLEDGEMENTS

I would like to express my grateful thanks to all those who have helped me with this book, especially Jenny Keal who has lain in muddy puddles, shivered in snow-bound tents, and hung over countless chasms to help me. She also took many of the photographs, helped type the manuscript and not least tried to curb some of my more outlandish excesses; Christine Bellamy for checking the manuscript; Hamish Brown, Hamid Hammou, Dr Madeleine Havard of the Marine Conservation Society, Andy Middleton, Linda Olson of the US National Parks Service and Colin Whittle; the many cavers who have given sterling assistance: Phil Coles, Jerry Cross, Huw Durban, Bill Gascoine, Phil Jayne, Paul Medhurst, Roy Morgan, with an especial thanks to Brent Durban for his amazing patience with the at times outrageous demands of the underground artist. I am also grateful to Cathy Gosling, Caroline Churton, Caroline Hill and Amzie Viladot at HarperCollins.

First published in 1995
by HarperCollins Publishers, London

© David Bellamy, 1995

David Bellamy asserts the moral right to be identified as the author of this work.

A catalogue record for this book is available from the British Library

ISBN 0 00 412709 9

Design Manager: Caroline Hill

Set in Optima, Hiroshige Book, Hiroshige Medium

Colour origination by Colourscan, Singapore
Produced by HarperCollins Hong Kong

The quotation on p.10 is taken from *Touch the Earth* by T.C. McLuhan and is reproduced by permission of Little, Brown & Co. (UK) Ltd.

Other books by David Bellamy:
The Wild Places of Britain, Painting in the Wild, David Bellamy's Watercolour Landscape Course, all published by HarperCollins; and *Images of the South Wales Mines,* published by Alan Sutton Ltd. *The Wild Coast of Britain* will be reissued by HarperCollins in 1996.

SAFETY WARNING
Many of the activities described in this book are *extremely hazardous.* Please get advice before indulging in any of them for the first time.

▶ SHELL CANYON, BIG HORN MOUNTAINS
455 × 305 mm
(18 × 12 in)

Previous pages:
EVENING LIGHT, GRAND TETONS, USA
255 × 340 mm
(10 × 13½ in)

CONTENTS

FOREWORD

As you read through this book, some of you will perhaps be curious as to how David has persuaded so many people to become his 'victims'. It is a complete mystery to me how he has managed to retain any friends at all. Of course, his family have little choice, but incredibly there is a whole army of apparently sensible people willing to join in his crazy games with little coercion, often more than once.

The words 'Let's have some fun today' from David are viewed with extreme suspicion. We all know by now that 'fun' to David must involve getting wet or muddy or both. It is also quite likely to involve being dangled on the end of a rope over a gaping chasm or a raging waterfall. Oddly enough, though, he is rarely the one who gets wet or terrified (his gear is always the cleanest when we get home) and usually he stands chuckling, with his camera or sketchbook ready. In fact, the threat of anyone slipping or getting into any sort of difficulty is far more likely to produce his camera than a helping hand. However, he calculates all the risks and is very aware of our safety, making sure, of course, that we don't know that. When he says 'This next bit looks interesting' there is usually an audible groan from the rest of us.

Many a Saturday morning is spent in trepidation, as we watch helmets, ropes, karabiners and inflatable rafts being loaded into the car. 'We are just going for a nice walk,' he says, with that smirk on his face and that twinkle in his eye that is impossible for him to disguise. At this stage I often get an unaccountable attack of common sense but almost always can be cured. In spite of the knowledge that we shall all come home with a few more bruises than we went with (last Saturday's bruises not having had time to heal) we all set off like lambs to the slaughter. How many times have I wished, as I hang upside down from a rope across a river in spate or lie in a 9 inch high passage, half full of water, deep in some cave system, while he takes a photo or sketches, that I was warm at home doing the ironing. Yet, next time he says 'Let's have some fun' we will all be there, having 'fun' (well, some of the time anyway).

Of course he is never going to grow up now, and no doubt I shall be abseiling in a wheelchair.

Jenny Keal

▶ LEWIS FALLS, WYOMING
215 × 295 mm
(8½ × 11½ in)
This has been painted on tinted paper, the colour of biscuits, and so the highlights have been brought out with the use of white gouache. I rarely use gouache on ordinary white paper.

INTRODUCTION

Many artists find themselves a comfortable seat, then paint what they can see, however low or awkward the angle. Comfort, and, at times, safety, must take second place for me.

Stern grey clouds began to blot out the ice-clad north face of the Ben. Spindrift raked the slopes of interminable whiteness as I climbed towards the summit of Càrn Mòr Dearg in the Central Highlands of Scotland. Another blizzard drove in, blotting out the distant peaks. The ferocious wind knocked me flat, and at the same time one of my crampons tore through my brand-new overtrousers, reducing them to rags at a stroke. Choking out a mouthful of soft snow, I clambered to my feet with the composure of a new-born foal, and lurched towards the welcoming embrace of a large rock. In the lee of the rock I sat gulping down warm tea from my flask.

Suddenly a break appeared in the whiteness, a window that revealed snow-capped distant peaks. Out came the sketchbook, and the pencil danced across the paper in an uncontrolled way. For once, nothing could go wrong – every stroke held the assurance of an accidental virtuoso. My icy, clod-like fingers were hopelessly out of control, yet nature was playing a game –

not only did she highlight the scene by framing it in a cloud window, but she also nudged the pencil and dropped snowflakes on the sketch, seemingly where it most mattered from a compositional point of view. Nature never ceases to amaze me. After witnessing such a display, I sang all the way to the summit.

Sketching in the wilds has always been my greatest love – the sheer enjoyment of being in rugged unspoilt places combined with the challenge of capturing an elusive or almost inaccessible subject sends a thrill

of exhilaration through me. Whether it is sunlight on a mountain crag, surf crashing against a rock arch, the force of white-water rapids pouring through a narrow defile, or spindrift pluming up over a snow-capped peak, elemental power can fire these places into dramatic settings that transcend the ordinary. These scenes, which less than 200 years ago evoked feelings of terror and superstition, have now become places of pleasure and wonder. Defoe, in his tour of Britain in the early eighteenth century gives us a clue to contemporary attitudes to the mountains in his description of Westmorland: 'Here we entered Westmoreland, a country eminent only for being the wildest, most barren and frightful of any that I have passed over in England, or even in Wales it self.'

◀ *The author sketching on horseback, Wyoming.*

▶ MOUNTAIN BOTHY
255 × 330 mm
(10 × 13 in)
This small stone hut stands against a savage backdrop of gloomy cliffs, in England's northern mountains.

◀ VULTURES, LOS
BARIOS, SPAIN
*The birds flew so low
that even fine detail
on their huge wings
was easily discernible.*

THE WILDERNESS EXPERIENCE

The variety of wild places is virtually
limitless, but in this book I concentrate on
those that have kindled my imagination.
The definition of wilderness tends to vary
with individuals – what is wild to some is
mild to others, and naturally weather and
season have a profound bearing on this.
Some fortunate individuals even see
wilderness within a cultivated hedgerow.
The North American Indian looked at it
rather differently to us.

*We did not think of the great open plains,
the beautiful rolling hills, and winding
streams with tangled growth, as 'wild'.
Only to the white man was nature a
'wilderness' and only to him was the land
'infested' with 'wild' animals and 'savage'
people. To us it was tame.*

Chief Standing Bear, Oglala Sioux

In a small way camping high in remote mountains brings us closer to such insights. Here we can absorb the atmosphere and beauty of the raw environment. Even the immediacy of rain beating on the tent fabric can generate a thrill. Sometimes I over-extend myself, and am caught descending the mountain in the dark after rejoicing in a glorious sunset on high ground. This last happened on Beinn Alliginn in the north of Scotland when we stood mesmerized by the sun setting over the distant Cuillin Hills of Skye. Suddenly it grew dark and we had a long way to go, glissading down steep snow slopes in Coir' nan Laogh to speed things up. After many tumbles we found ourselves below the snow line. By this time there was little light, but the moon shone high above the silver crest of Spidean A'Choire Leith. Several potential sketches tantalized me, the lack of detail exerting a powerful edge to the mood of the scenery, but with our lateness likely to result in a Mountain Rescue call-out we had to keep going.

◄ HIGH ATLAS,
MOROCCO
240 × 340 mm
(9½ × 13½ in)
This dwelling was caught partly in sunlight, dwarfed by the Djebel Toubkal massif, the highest mountain in North Africa.
In the collection of
Miss Sue Dixson

TOPOGRAPHICAL VARIETY

The book has been arranged with chapters covering a certain type of terrain, such as deserts or rivers. Obviously there tends to be a certain amount of overlap – the River Nile flows through deserts, and gorges are usually found in mountainous areas, for instance. Behind each sketch lies a tale or an adventure. Often humour is a strong ingredient. You simply cannot go into these places and not experience danger, discomfort, pain, humility, laughter or absolute amazement at the beauty around you. Whether mountaineering or painting, in the race to the summit we should not lose sight of the delights of the climb.

The search in sketching the sublime draws me into all sorts of terrain, where often a mental battle ensues – common sense tells me it is too dangerous to continue, yet I am desperate to get into position for the sketch. My thoughts range in multi-levels, the most basic being the 'responsible' one urging me not to be silly. Against this is the back-to-childhood daring, fanning my urges for excitement. These thoughts intermingle several times, to be replaced by yet another level: 'I must carry on, even if it is dangerous, as it is a challenge.' Against that my mind remonstrates that 'you've given it a good try, but it is impossible.'

All these thoughts often come to nothing, because in the end I suddenly switch off, think perhaps of the colours or textures of the rock I am clinging to, and make the move without thought, or conscious decision!

◀ DRAGON'S LAIR, PORTH TRE-WEN. PEMBROKESHIRE 240 × 150 mm (9½ × 6 in) *This rock is evil – razor-sharp and crumbling at the slightest touch. Best seen on a murky day.*

David Bellamy

◄ BLEAKLOW,
DERBYSHIRE
225 × 330 mm
(9 × 13 in)

Yet our over-civilized society seems forever trying to reduce this natural wildness. 'Forget the map and compass – let's take a mobile telephone and ring the Mountain Rescue Team at the first hint of danger, mist, storm or panic,' is often the attitude. If we seek new horizons we must have the courage to leave behind the safety of the harbour. Anyone venturing into the hills, out to sea or down a cave should be properly equipped mentally, as well as physically. Bridges, roads and visitor centres have no place in true wilderness. Not only do they encourage the inexperienced into uncompromising terrain, and contradict the wilderness concept, but they are eyesores completely out of keeping in wild areas.

Given the pace of life, turning to the wild places to recharge our emotional batteries is essential. Towns and cities grow larger and uglier by the minute, and children brought up in these tortured places rarely experience the true magic of nature. To feel warm rock in your hand, see dewdrops on a mountain saxifrage, or hear the call of an oystercatcher on a remote beach gladdens the heart and melts away the worries of life. Transforming these experiences into paintings is, to me, one of the voyages of discovery, of both nature and myself.

SKETCHING METHODS

All the sketches in the book were done on the spot. Some will show rain spots, mud, effects of watercolour freezing, and so on. Many are carried out in watercolour, to capture the atmosphere, or in pencil, water-soluble pencil or charcoal. On one occasion I improved a pencil sketch with a soggy tea-bag! Out on location I support these sketches with photographs and notes. From this source material the paintings are then worked up in the studio at home, injecting the mood, sky effects or lighting from one scene into another when necessary. Sometimes I change a scene considerably between sketch and painting. This approach needs much visualization combined with a deep understanding of atmospheric effects and the character of the scene being portrayed. My best work is created, I feel,

where I have allowed the role of visualizer to predominate. I have been told that some paintings are far removed from the real thing, but then I always blame the weather!

Notes on how a number of the sketches and paintings were achieved have been included, for those who are interested in the manner in which the work evolved. The feature spreads show in greater depth how certain subjects have been tackled. Caving, in many ways, demands a different approach to sketching. Apart from the obvious problems of lighting, it is exceptionally hard on equipment, which also needs to be kept dry in deep pools and underwater sections. Speed is essential when sketching in a wild location with several companions. Time-cutting techniques are vital, but those such as belaying someone with the rope between your teeth while sketching, are non-starters!

◄ BERBER LORRY

▲ WATERFALL, JOYCE'S RIVER, CONNEMARA
This rough watercolour sketch was a demonstration for a course group, and reveals how rain spots on the wet watercolour enhance the work considerably. Perhaps I should do all my watercolours in the rain …

▶ BISON IN THE COTTONWOODS
420 × 560 mm
(16½ × 22 in)

ADVENTURES OF YOUR OWN

For those who wish to take up any of the activities described in the text, the Appendix on pages 124–6 will guide you to suitable places and organizations. Also included is information on suitable equipment, art materials and other useful items. Please take heed of the warnings. Many of the activities are dangerous, and the newcomer needs expert guidance, so do make sure you seek out help and advice before trying anything of this nature.

Walking is only one manner of reaching the scenery – I also use canoes, rafts, ropes, swimming, wading, horses, bicycles and other means at times. Horses, for example, are a marvellous way of seeing the countryside, as you can cover so much ground and not tire as easily as when walking. Although I do sketch from the horse's back, I prefer to dismount to do a proper job, as the horse usually moves around once the reins are slack. Riding in the Wind River Range in the American West was the highlight of my limited equestrian experience. I ended up trying to lure a rattlesnake out of a bush so that I could sketch it. Sadly my snake charming failed abysmally!

On many of the sketching expeditions I travelled alone, sometimes out of necessity, sometimes because nobody wanted to subject themselves to the sheer discomfort, danger and diabolical conditions, or perhaps simply because a better job could be done by working on my own. Jenny, my partner, joins me on a great number of the trips, despite an early setback on Bleaklow,

◄ *Jenny in Peat Grough, Bleaklow, Derbyshire.*

▼ BOW FELL FROM MICKLEDEN, LAKE DISTRICT

in the Peak District, when she became bogged down in glutinous black peat. She and many of our caving friends have been extremely helpful, understanding and patient in putting up with my often outrageous demands, at times in considerable discomfort, all in the cause of artistic expression. I cannot thank them enough.

CONSERVATION

Over the years the landscape has provided me with a great deal of pleasure and, of course, my livelihood. As a consequence I take every opportunity to put something back into the countryside, by working closely at times with conservation bodies such as the Campaign for the Protection of Rural Wales, The Marine Conservation Society and The John Muir Trust. Art and nature have a natural affinity, each invoking a powerful mood and emotion in those who seek out a more than superficial relationship. I think there are far too many threats to the countryside to stand back and let them happen. The British National Parks are treated abysmally by government and big business, whose accountants seem unable to tell the difference between a marsh flower and a lump of concrete! They cannot see beauty in a pool of mud. One of the worst examples is the Cwm Dyli pipeline built by the electricity board up the east slopes of the Snowdon massif. This desecrates one of Wales' most magnificent views. Sadly the electricity industry has ravaged so much of the beauty of Snowdonia with their ghastly pylons. There

are alternatives, but unless voices are raised against these atrocities our countryside will continue to be spoilt in this way. Surely man is now sufficiently advanced to put materialism secondary to caring for our resources. The underhand practices so often perpetrated by man leave me cold. We are no longer in touch with the earth.

▲ LOCH CLAIR, TORRIDON, SCOTLAND
225 × 320 mm
(9 × 12½ in)

TIDE WATCHING

The hypnotic spell woven by surging surf against the wave-torn fabric of the wild coasts, has always held me entranced. But however bad a sailor he might be, the true artist of the sea is duty bound to immerse himself in it.

◀ ANDY MIDDLETON
CANOEING IN RAMSEY
SOUND, WALES
320 × 455 mm
(12½ × 18 in)

▶ BULLSLAUGHTER
BAY, PEMBROKESHIRE
305 × 510 mm
(12 × 20 in)

Huge walls of wild waves as high as a line of charging elephants bore down on our kayaks, threatening to swamp us. Jenny held on grimly to my canoe, mindful that if we were torn apart all I would have to paddle with was a medium-grade Karisma pencil!

SEA PORTRAIT

A wave crashed over us. We rose on the crest, then swooped down after top canoeist Andy Middleton into the trough beyond.

Exhilaration turned to trepidation as another wall of water hit us. After the initial shock, and amazed that we were still upright, I concentrated hard on sketching the portrait of Andy, owner of the Twr y Felin Outdoor Centre at St Davids on the Welsh coast. With all this effort results had to be forthcoming! Sketching a moving target is a considerable challenge, especially when you are being completely swamped at

regular intervals and expecting to capsize at any moment. Achieving a likeness of Andy's general stance and the manner in which the churning water crashed over him and his kayak, held my total attention. Within seconds we were swept half a mile up Ramsey Sound on the wild Pembrokeshire coast, hurtling towards the notorious Bitches reef. Then Andy hauled us out of the wild current and into calmer waters, just as we were beginning to enjoy the experience.

Paddling backwards and towing our kayaks was not the easiest of manoeuvres for Andy, but it was the only way I could capture a lifelike action portrait of him. Jenny's role had been vital – without stability my sketches would have resembled the charted movements of a grasshopper dipped in liquid graphite. We paddled back to our original position and prepared for another run. Again Andy backed us into the

heaving seas. We shot up, down and into the frothing water on an aquatic switchback, until pulled out once more.

By now Andy was pretty tired, so with the main purpose accomplished – two soggy scribbled sketches stuffed into a mapcase – we paddled back up the sound close under the cliffs, edging in and out of sea caves, fitting lairs from which the mythical Greek giant Polyphemus might emerge to vent his wrath. Sunlight danced across the water, reflecting moving patterns of silver streamers into multicoloured rocks. Our kayaks cleaved through the iridescent, almost luminous, green water under soaring rock arches, pausing beneath amethyst cliffs for me to do more portrait work in calmer surroundings. Back at St Justinian's, from where we had launched, we hauled the kayaks out of the water, exhausted, but exhilarated by a marvellous afternoon.

COASTAL TRAVERSING

Canoeing is a superb way of exploring wild coastlines, as the walker on the clifftop path misses so much of the dramatic cliff architecture below. When no canoe or boat is available, one way around this problem is by coastal traversing or coasteering. This exciting activity can either be done 'dry' by keeping just above the waterline, or 'wet' by wearing a wetsuit and jumping in the water where necessary. Needless to say, either method is inherently dangerous, as you have to maintain a close watch on both tide and sea state. Even a fairly calm sea can cause horrific problems and the ability to swim is a definite advantage!

Along most rugged coastlines it is relatively easy to spot potentially rewarding locations for traversing. Rock arches, pinnacles, secluded coves and dramatic rock formations can often be spotted from the path, but usually they are seen at an awkward angle. By getting in close at sea level the drama of the site is accentuated and the perspective from a sketching point of view greatly improved. Reconnaissance sketches and long-range photographs taken on the walk help in planning future traversing expeditions.

▲ WILD SURF,
ST BRIDES,
PEMBROKESHIRE
A rough two-minute sketch carried out with a water-soluble pencil in boisterous conditions. The waves swamped me up to waist level and provided the water for the sketch.

▼ ROCK ARCH,
ST NONS,
PEMBROKESHIRE
We edged into the arch in kayaks, rasping up and down against the sides as deep-green waves caught the craft.

◄ ROCKS AT
BROAD HAVEN,
PEMBROKESHIRE

ABSEILING TO SKETCH

Where there is no route down to a spectacular scene, the only course is to abseil into a sketching position. In many cases this is straightforward, but now and then if the landing point cannot be seen from the top it could prove embarrassing – falling off the end of a rope is both inelegant and damaging to sketching equipment. Landing in deep water can have the same effect. Climbing back up is another matter. From above little idea can be obtained of how difficult this might be, so jammers are a necessity. These useful light alloy devices clamp onto the rope, enabling you to climb up it.

SKETCHING IN DIFFICULT LOCATIONS

When I come across a subject in a difficult position like this, if I cannot get to it immediately, I make a note of the state of the tide, study possible approach routes, take photographs through a powerful zoom lens, and draw a reconnaissance sketch or diagram to help lay plans for a future mission. I then return at the chosen hour suitably equipped.

I decided to abseil down onto a narrow rib of rock that ran out some 60 metres parallel with the cliff, with an almost perfect viewpoint of the cavern. I had to tackle it at low tide, as the rocks that connected the rib to the cliff were under water after about one-third of an incoming tide. I chose a sunny morning at 7.30 a.m. for the venture, abseiling down with my equipment secure in a drysack, essential as the rib was constantly being liberally sprayed with surf.

The view of the cavern was magnificent, and the lighting just right, with the sun above Caldey Island in the distance. I sketched furiously, mindful that the tide was on its way in, especially as I could not see from the end of the rib if the connecting rock was still above water. Once completed, I returned to the bottom of the cliff and climbed back up. I had taken the precaution of carrying jammers along in case I could not climb back so that I could use them to climb up the rope itself. Rule one in these situations concerns safety – make sure you can get back! Rule two concerns sketching – choose your moment carefully for both lighting and tide level.

▲ *Traversing the rock rib at Lydstep, Pembrokeshire. The escape route is out of the picture on the left.*

▲ *The author about to get wet.*

◄ THE ORIGINAL SKETCH CARRIED OUT ON THE ROCK RIB

► CAVERN AT LYDSTEP, PEMBROKESHIRE
205 × 305 mm
(8 × 12 in)

▲ SKOMAR TOWER,
LYDSTEP
510 × 45 mm
(20 × 17½ in)
This is Pembrokeshire

at its best, a scene
that can only be
reached by wading
through the surf on a
low spring tide.

WHERE DID I PUT THE TRIDENT?

Ideally I like to arrive in front of my subject
an hour or so before low tide. Often this
involves little more than walking down to a
remote beach and scrambling across rocks
to the chosen point, but at times there is a
need to place a fixed rope, abseil, swim or
wade across sections of deeper water. This
happened one December afternoon at
Lydstep in Pembrokeshire, where there are
several impressive caverns in the limestone
cliffs. Unknown to me, this happened to be
a spring tide where the water was
exceptionally low.

Telling Catherine, my young daughter,
to stay high up the beach, I charged fully
clothed into the surf, with my sketching gear
in an old rucksack. Rounding the cliff to my
right, in deeper water, a wave hit me above
the waist, causing me to gasp at the sudden
cold shock. Ahead lay my subject – a great
soaring archway with the spectacular
silhouette of Skomar Tower seen through it.
A short wade brought me into a tiny cove
and onto a small patch of sand.

The scene completely took my breath
away. Skomar Tower rose high up on the far
cliff, framed by the savage splendour of the
magnificent rock arch. I sketched
frenetically, keeping a wary eye on the
incoming tide. Returning would be more
risky, but the scenery made the risk
worthwhile. Late afternoon sunshine cast
long shadows across the sand, and glanced
off rock faces. So much complicated detail
needed at least an hour to render properly,
but my brief interlude on this lovely shore
could only span minutes.

Finishing the sketch, I stowed away the gear and braced myself for my return. The tide had come in some distance and my plunge into the water induced even greater gasps than my first wetting. Surging out, waist-deep, I needed to wade some 40 metres out to sea before turning parallel with the cliff on my left. A wave caught me chest-high, momentarily unbalancing me. Realizing that a few more like that could completely submerge me, I thrust forward at full power before the next wave hit me. It crashed into me sideways, hitting my rucksack and spinning me round like a skittle. This position was more vulnerable, so as the third wave approached I swung straight into it to both shield the rucksack and give myself a better chance to hold firm. Another wave, a gasp and the beach was mine.

As I rejoined my daughter an elderly couple watched from the far side of the shore. How insane it must have seemed to them, this fully clothed figure walking out of the wild December sea with no sign of a boat or anything but cliffs and lively surf. If only I had a trident to add to the mystique, to emerge like some latter-day Neptune, 'the waves bound beneath me as a steed', as Byron put it. Hand in hand, Catherine and I danced laughing up the beach to some puzzled looks.

KEELHAULING
These days, for wet traverses and swimming to sketching positions I generally wear a wetsuit. Constantly jumping in and out of the water, especially during the colder months, can be extremely chilling,

particularly when there is a complicated sketch to be done after immersion. Even with a reasonably calm sea, in places where you have to clamber up rocks out of deep water, the swell alone can rasp you across barnacles as effective as any keelhauling!

▲ LITTLE SKELLIG,
EIRE
330 × 495 mm
(13 × 19½ in)
The large amount of gannet droppings on its peaks almost gave this small island the appearance of a giant iceberg, enhancing its visual attraction if not its physical one. The sky at times was black with birds. Although the far end of the island was visible I realized that a little atmosphere over the right-hand side would improve the composition. The scene was sketched from Skellig Michael, the larger of the two islands off the coast of Kerry.

DAGGERS OF ROCK

Choosing a location for a water-level traverse needs great care. Some traverses involve lengthy stretches of coastline, linking several beaches to seek out possible subjects for sketching; others are short escapades with a planned objective.

One hot summer's day I decided to attempt a descent to Traeth Gwyndwn-mawr, a beach in North Pembrokeshire, lying below high cliffs of shattered precipitous rock. I wanted to sketch at close hand the evil-looking daggers of rock which rose from the beach. With Catherine, then thirteen years old and with quite a lot of experience of coastal traversing, I walked along the clifftop to assess the best route down.

First I had to hack a path through bracken nearly two metres high, below which a grassy shelf sloped towards sheer unstable cliffs. My aim was to locate a nose where two cliffs met at right angles, and here I found a less steep route that was stepped, leading down to a rocky promontory at sea level. Catherine roped up and went down the cliff, as I belayed her from above; then I joined her. Nearby a jellyfish hung in deep water.

We traversed to the left above an inlet, the cliff becoming steeper until we could get no further without falling off. I lassooed a prominent rock above, catching it at about the tenth attempt, and then pulled myself up the rope to secure it. I then jumped into the water, as an overhang prevented us climbing down. The fixed rope would help get us back up. Catherine came across the inlet on my shoulder. Then we scrambled along the far side, and up over a rib, high above deep water.

Suddenly, I slipped on greasy rock, just managing to prevent myself plunging down the face. A dodgy traverse led across the face of the cliff, the almost vertical bedding and friable sections of the face providing a sporting obstacle about ten metres above the sea, with lethally sharp rocks below. I kept close to my daughter, guiding her all the way until we reached a friendly gully. Up we went until it ended in a sheer drop 12 metres down the far side.

◄ TRAETH GWYNDWN-MAWR, PEMBROKESHIRE

▲ *Catherine, my daughter, on a tricky traverse.*

► CAVALL BERNAT RIDGE, MALLORCA
240 × 330 mm
(9½ × 13 in)
To the north the ridge drops sheer for about 300 metres (1000 feet) into the sea. The limestone has a vicious cutting edge, but provides a good grip for climbing.

◄ CARN LES BOEL,
CORNWALL
215 × 305 mm
(8½ × 12 in)

► SEVERN ESTUARY
FROM THE GWENT
LEVELS
165 × 330 mm
(6½ × 13 in)

Without a rope such a descent would be difficult, but by linking two slings and a short length of 5 mm rope, I had enough to protect Catherine's descent to halfway down, below which she said it looked impossible. Securing the 'rope', I descended past her and found a route down to the beach, and she quickly joined me. Once across the beach we found a suitable sketching site and began work on the rocks,

at the same time eating a picnic lunch. With the tide now turning we could not afford to spend too long there.

Stopping to carry out a sketch in places where there is little chance of escape and the tide is rising absolutely fractures the nerves. On my own the decision is easier, but when you are responsible for the safety of others, sketching needs to take second place. Every pencil stroke has to count.

It is amazing how the mind is concentrated on getting down on paper only the essential elements of the scene. Such experiences are highly recommended for artists who wish to improve their critical observation. To snatch a composition from the very jaws of disaster does, I admit, give immense satisfaction. Perhaps it is the closest thing that visual art comes to being an Olympic sport!

IN DEEP WATER

Time was running out. After two sketches I hastily packed my gear. We climbed back up the vertical cliff and across the tricky traverse without any problems. At the inlet, where the tide had risen waist high, I slid into the water. Again Catherine came across on my shoulder, high enough to ensure a fairly easy scramble onto the rock, with the aid of the fixed rope. However, I found it difficult to climb out of the deep water. Although I had prussick loops – two short lengths of thin rope knotted onto the climbing rope to facilitate ascent – they failed to help me up the rope. Barely above the water level, I pulled myself up, but the angle of the rope caused me to pendulum across the cliff, leaving behind large quantities of skin from my forearm as it rasped against rough rock. Catherine did not know whether to laugh or cry. In the end I gave up on the loops and waded into deeper water, then hauled myself up partly using the rope and partly using rock holds. Once on safe ground we scrambled up the cliff and I did another sketch.

IMPROVING THE BACKDROP

Often I find that the environment in which I sketch wildlife simply does not suit the composition of my painting. This scene is one such case, where the seal was lying on a rather bland-looking rock. A change was essential to create a suitable backdrop, though not too busy, as I wanted the seal to be the centre of interest.

Where a considerable alteration is to take place I first draw some rough thumbnail sketches, working out my ideas before committing myself to watercolour paper. Failure to do this usually results in erasing a lot of pencil lines, or even tearing up the sheet. Experimenting with different sizes also helps me to achieve a satisfactory composition.

Normally I like to make the centre of interest of the painting – in this case the seal – stand out clearly by simplifying the surrounding detail. However, there is always an exception to the rule, and here I wanted to play a little trick. Seals are not always easy to spot when lying on a rocky foreshore, so I felt it would be an interesting exercise to camouflage this one, almost losing it in the background. As a result, some people looking at this painting did not even see the seal!

A great deal of patience is normally required to obtain good reference material on a seal, as these animals are naturally shy. In the water little more than the head and neck is visible, although looking directly down on the seal in shallow water reveals more. I use binoculars, or a 200 mm camera lens through which I can sketch, albeit with difficulty. Seals are usually best observed from boats.

Marrying various sketches, perhaps from completely different locations is a fascinating challenge, though fraught with potential pitfalls. The character of the scene must be retained to achieve authenticity, no matter how many sketches are involved, as are more obvious aspects such as keeping the direction of the light uniform.

misty background cliffs

critical area

run-off

lively surf

highlight or camouflage?

▲ ROUGH THUMBNAIL SKETCH FOR SEAL BACKGROUND
Once I had an idea of the sort of background that worked best, I searched through my sketches for detail that closely matched the thumbnail sketch.

▲ Bear Rock,
Hartland, Devon
305 × 455 mm
(12 × 18 in)

WRECKS AND ROCKS

One of my favourite parts of the coast in north Devon is the Hartland area. Here savage ribs of rock jut out into the Atlantic like rows of jagged shark's teeth. These ribs, composed of tilted beds of sandstone, are more resistant than the softer mudstone sandwiched between the layers, and have claimed many shipwrecks over the years, evidence of which still lies on the beaches. By getting down on the beaches the rock structure is laid bare before you. The stretch between Hartland Quay and Damehole Point provides sustained interest without too much difficulty at low tide. Even so, care is needed – the sea must always be regarded with great respect. A fall resulting in a broken ankle could prove disastrous.

I left Hartland Quay one glorious morning, not entirely sure whether to be glad of the fine weather with excellent lighting for sketching the rocks, or annoyed at the lack of a storm to provide an atmosphere in keeping with the wild surroundings. Above Warren beach the cliffs soar to a spectacular 76 metres (250 feet), as unstable as a pile of empty milk bottles. The tall pinnacle of Bear Rock at the far end provided a noble focal point for a sketch. Variegated colours and textures on the rock excited me – it just had to be a watercolour. This was sketching at its best: superb light, exciting shapes and at a place too inaccessible for crowds to gather. An oystercatcher joined me briefly. Beyond this my route led through a rock arch, another shapely subject for those infatuated by rock scenery.

As my line of communication with safety lengthened, my sketches became more rapid. Dyer's Lookout, with its imposing cliffs jutting out, was the next point of interest. Once through the gap between the cliff and a large crag, by working round the edge of deep pools, I reached the beach beyond that runs all the way round to Damehole Point, with an escape to the coast path near Blackpool Mill.

Closer to Damehole Point lie the rusting parts of a wreck, including a huge anchor. This is all that remains of the *Hoche*, a French steamship bound from Rouen to Cardiff, which ran aground on 1 July 1882.

▲ DAMEHOLE POINT, DEVON

► SUNSET OVER A SEA-LOCH, MULL
190 × 295 mm
(7½ × 11½ in)

Happily, the crew reached shore safely, and for one member it was the second time he had been shipwrecked at Hartland!

Just below Damehole Point I wriggled into a narrow through cave to an open chamber beyond. On three sides rose cliffs but on the fourth the floor dropped down to a deep pool. The choice lay in getting wet, retreating or climbing the cliffs. I chose the latter, enjoying the scramble to the top of the cliff above the pool and descending an even steeper face on the far side. Here my trip ended, high on a grassy slope sketching birds and cliffs, while making the most of a picnic lunch.

COASTAL POLLUTION

Increasingly our wild coastlines are under threat from development, both on land and at sea. As a patron of the Marine Conservation Society this concerns me deeply. Oil exploration is now taking place off the Pembrokeshire coast – a National Park with a spectacular coastline and a Marine Nature Reserve at Skomer Island. Oil spillage is bad enough around Milford Haven at the best of times, but this development will exacerbate the problem. So often when sitting on rocks you are only too aware of oil.

Even the oil exploration process itself appears to be harmful, the seismic shootings apparently causing distress to dolphins and fish. Arguments put forward by the Government that not enough is known about these effects bear little support. More funding must be put into research on what is happening to the fragile marine eco-system before we continue to destroy the fish and bird life of our seas. Euripides said that 'The sea washes away all the ills of mankind', but under the current sustained attack by developers, it seems that only when man completely destroys himself will this be true.

SECRET GORGES

These glittering ribbons of the fellsides are ignored by most sane people in their quest to reach the summit, but for the artist they hold treasures more precious than the crown jewels.

Water crashing over savage rock scenery provides the two elements that excite me most, whether painting or traversing. This is landscape that can be tackled in all kinds of weathers – even when the river runs full with snow-melt. I often deliberately seek gorges out when they are flowing fast and furious, for the added buzz.

In high winds or bad weather gorges afford shelter, and indeed come into their own in mist conditions when panoramic sketching is a lost cause. When scrambling up gorges, the intention is to remain as dry as possible, although this rarely turns out to be the case!

GILL CLIMBING

Throughout the world there are truly spectacular gorges, such as the Grand Canyon in the USA, or the Torrente de Pareis in Mallorca where in places, although only a few metres wide, the gorge's sides are hundreds of metres deep. We traversed the Torrente de Pareis when it was bone dry, but although magnificent, for me it lacked the sparkle of cascading water that may be found in the gills of the English Lake District.

In fact the Lake District is one of the best places to pursue this masochistic pastime. Here, there is a strong tradition for gill climbing, where as a sport the idea is to keep as close to the water as possible without getting wet or falling in. Hemmed in on both sides by sheer cliffs for much of the way, and trying to avoid the stream, the gorge scrambler is presented with a series of formidable obstacles, some of Herculean dimensions. Much clambering is required, often up waterfalls, which can be highly entertaining for spectators. Paintings in such places are hard won, their pleasure multiplied by memories of splashing water silvered in dappled sunlight, of rich, moss-covered boulders and a sense of being in your own private Arcadia. Here the storms of life are forgotten, and even the most abominable sketch seems to be a masterpiece. For a brief moment the artist becomes part of nature.

Dungeon Ghyll in Langdale is an outstanding climb up a necklace of sparkling pools amidst sublime scenery. In freezing winter, when transformed by enormous icicles hanging like silver stalactites, the gill affords a marvellous spectacle of studies for any artist happy to brave the cold. Here, I once dropped an ice-axe through a hole in an iced-up pool, and provided much entertainment for my companions as I tried to retrieve it, eventually crashing through the ice!

▲ ICE FORMATIONS,
DUNGEON GHYLL,
LAKE DISTRICT
240 × 150 mm
(9½ × 6 in)

▶WINTER CHASM,
BEN NEVIS
240 × 270 mm
(9½ × 10½ in)

ROMANTIC GYMNASTICS

One April, while we were running a painting course in Elterwater, Cumbria, Jenny indicated that she would like to go for a romantic riverside stroll on our free afternoon. Nearby, at Tilberthwaite, with the mist clearing, I suggested we walk up beside the gill. After climbing two waterfalls and actually crossing the gill several times Jenny began to query my definition of the word 'romantic' – to her this route seemed more akin to an assault course! We persevered until, on rounding a corner, we came to an enormous gash in great black cliffs, vertical and sinister looking. Here, even on the sunniest day, dark shadows lurk. In all Cumbria, this is perhaps the most fitting place to perpetrate some grisly deed!

Jenny did not agree that it would be a jolly wheeze to traverse the gorge with few holds on slimy rock above a raging torrent. If I wanted to do it she would watch.

The first section involved a short climb on fairly unstable rock, followed by a descent into a shallow part of the stream. As it deepened I climbed onto a narrow ledge, cursing the heavy rucksack on my back. A traverse led along the side of the gorge barely a metre above the fast-flowing torrent, which was becoming increasingly too deep for comfort. Now came the tricky bit – my body hovered out directly above the white water, as I placed most of my weight on my arms, ready to commit myself to a lunge to safety. With a sigh of relief I landed on firm rock.

But everything behind me now paled into insignificance compared to the horrors I saw

ahead. My heart sank. Greasy, slimy rocks, sloped downwards almost vertically towards a deep pool. The first part looked impossible, with worse to come higher up, so if I managed to reach that far a retreat would present a nightmare. There would be no protection. The right-hand wall fell vertical, smooth as a sow's backside, and curved towards the waterfall which crashed down with tremendous power into the pool.

▶ PONTSARN AND TAF FECHAN, SOUTH WALES

◀ *Bellamy making an easy move look difficult.*

▶ WATERFALL,
TILBERTHWAITE GILL,
CUMBRIA
380 × 255 mm
(15 × 10 in)
To the left of the
waterfall is the
horrific greasy rock
wall that I had to
climb to escape from
this dank and dire
prison.

CLIMBING GREASE

I decided to give it a try, not expecting to get beyond the first section. Crossing the stream was no problem at the bottom of the pool, where rocks broke the surface. I reached the first obstacle – a rocky rib projecting down into the water. Trying to get my leg over the rib and firmly planted on a good hold beyond was easier said than done – like trying to mount a rearing stallion without falling backwards. Hand holds were virtually non-existent – the rock felt as though it had been liberally coated with axle grease. Slowly, with an ungainly arc, my right leg straddled the rib, ending with a sudden surge towards the foothold, which steadied my tottering balance. So far so good. My right hand searched for holds, but found nothing. All the time water dripped from above, making me almost as wet as if I had jumped in.

Holding the position was tiring, and I decided to retreat so that both legs stood to the left of the rib, then pondered an alternative approach. Starting from lower down might work. Again I swung my right leg over the rib, placing my foot on a scant hold centimetres above the water. Then, thrusting forwards and upwards, I brought my left leg over beside my right while my right hand simply balanced without providing a hold.

Scrambling up easier holds to a safer position, high above the deepest part of the pool, I gazed down at the foaming water. Thoughts of trying to swim weighed down with a heavy rucksack flashed through my mind. I pulled myself together. Be positive.

The next move was tricky, forcing me to hang out, highly exposed, over the torrent to negotiate an awkward bulge with only grease for a hold. Pushing all my weight onto the sloping rock with the palm of my hand, I used momentum to propel myself to the next safe spot.

At this point little would have induced me to retreat – going down that greased rock wall would have been asking to end up at the bottom of the pool. I heaved myself up with my right arm, thankfully realizing that the climb was almost over. Then, with a yell of triumph, I jumped down into the stream well above the waterfall. I had made it.

MISSION ACCOMPLISHED

I walked up the gill, from here an easy route through boulders, and stopped to sketch the scene with mist-shrouded snow slopes above. Dense vegetation covered the vertical walls of the ravine. I finished the sketch and made for the easiest-looking point to climb up the steep rockface, a drop of about 25 metres. At first all went well. Up a grassy bank, followed by a precipitous climb with good holds on rock and tree roots interspersed with earth and vegetation. But, some four metres from the lip, the holds ran out: and the odd clump of grass inspired little faith. Pondering the situation, I removed the rucksack and secured it to a tree root before extracting a rope, something we always carry on a romantic stroll! Taking a deep breath, I lassooed a tree-trunk directly above, tied the rucksack onto one end of the rope and, grasping the rope, pulled myself up the last few metres to the top, where I gratefully hugged the tree.

Shortly afterwards I rejoined Jenny who was still pondering over the definition of a romantic stroll.

PLANT LIFE

Most of the gills in Oxendale, at the head of Langdale, Cumbria, lead up towards Pike O'Blisco or Crinkle Crags, providing a sporting way of climbing these tops. This way you can avoid the crowds on the paths and the scenery is usually superior. Climbing the gorge sides can often cause damage, so it is important to choose a route that considers the environment as well as safety. Being either in the water or on firm rock means you cause less erosion, although you should take care not to damage the luxuriant plant life that decorates these gills.

▲ BRUNT GILL, LAKE DISTRICT

► *Jenny traversing Browney Gill with Colin Whittle, one of our painting friends.*

Such richness of natural habitats is becoming rare in toxic Britain, and it is imperative that we conserve what little we have left.

Dampness keeps the mosses and ferns an intense green, and many abstract paintings can be visualized in the intermix of rock, vegetation and moisture. The bright splashes of intense colour form a delightful break in an otherwise sombre environment.

On days when clouds hang low over the mountains, the gills offer salvation to the day, for by deliberately seeking out the misty upper reaches, the artist is well rewarded. Background crags get lost in the mist. Mysterious shapes come and go behind the stern imagery of hard-edged rock, and even a small cascade breathes a gleam of hope to an austere landscape, giving the artist a ready-made focal point on which to resolve the composition. Here, even the inexperienced painter cannot fail to accomplish a pleasing work, with nature giving so much guidance. Getting out and working directly from nature is the best way to learn the secrets of the artist, and gill climbing on misty days hands over the composition on a plate.

▶ TILBERTHWAITE GILL, CUMBRIA
This autumnal scene interested me for the colours and lovely shapes of the trees, lost in places and strongly etched in others.

WORKING ON A LARGE PAINTING

Translating a small pencil sketch into a painting of this size is a sobering exercise. Admittedly a photograph helped to provide more detail, but in a specific scene like this it is essential that all the detail is in keeping with the character of the place. Ideally a larger sketch would have been better, but I had little time.

In the final painting I decided to leave in the figure to give a sense of scale, although the trees also do this to a degree. With such a large area to fill I felt a reasonably interesting sky would enhance the painting. Additionally a certain amount of counterchange where the sky abuts hills subtly adds variation. Planning the execution of washes in such a complicated painting needs deliberate care as, once committed, any changes in a watercolour may be impossible.

To create a sense of spaciousness I have made the figure and the trees smaller in relation to the overall size of the painting, than they are in the original sketch. By using a full imperial sheet of watercolour paper this has made the task easier. Some subjects lend themselves to large-scale work, but of course it is essential to record sufficient detail when doing the sketch.

Naturally it takes longer to paint a large watercolour when there is so much detail, and there is a danger of the quality slipping if tiredness creeps in. I therefore try to carry out the work in phases, stopping the moment I feel myself becoming stale. Another day and I am eager to continue the painting afresh.

▲ Pencil Sketch for Painting of Scwd Gwladys

▶ Scwd Gwladys, Brecon Beacons
535 × 660 mm
(21 × 26 in)

CLIMBING A WATERFALL

Crinkle Gill, which I climbed with two friends, Robert Hart and Kevin Myers, one winter's day, provides a neat little scramble up a waterfall, out of a large chamber near the top limit of the actual gill. This means getting a little wet, something which Robert tries to avoid like the plague. All the way up he had taken the easier options, but this one he could not avoid – or so he thought! I scrambled up first, after some deliberation about the best route, and Kevin followed.

Robert felt the need for a rope, however, and produced one with a flourish. He threw it up to me, and tied on. As Robert began his ascent Kevin chuckled and indicated to me that a path led up behind the crag to the right of the waterfall. We kept quiet as Robert retreated, seeking an easier line. He then decided to take a run at it, something rare in the annals of rock climbing. Both Kevin and I waited in open-mouthed anticipation as Robert rocketed towards the waterfall and leapt upwards amidst a great spray of water. Somehow it did not work, and once again Robert was back at the foot of the fall, only a bit wetter. I suggested a more deliberate approach, as belaying at such speeds was quite challenging. This time Robert was more methodical, and with a tight rope he gradually reached the top of the waterfall, while bemoaning the lack of suitable waterfalls on which to practise in

▶ CRINKLE GILL,
LAKE DISTRICT
330 × 255 mm
(13 × 10 in)

Northamptonshire. He was not amused when we pointed out the easy alternative ascent!

'WELLIE SAFARIS'

The misfortunes of others in these situations, of course, can provide marvellous entertainment for the rest of the party. Gill climbing is ideal for this, as are what we call 'wellie safaris'. These tend to be in gorges less steep than the fellside gills, where we wear Wellington boots to stem the ingress of water for as long as possible. The scenery is extremely inspiring – there is nothing like being in the middle of the river to get the optimum view for sketching a subject!

One memorable occasion in the Clydach Gorge of South Wales, when the river was in spate, provided an entertaining two and a half hours. We only covered about 300 metres, and afterwards it took us all of ten minutes to return along the path! This was a family occasion, when our teenage daughters Jo, Caroline and Catherine joined Jenny and me in an aquatic ramble. The girls found their small wellingtons were quickly filled by the fast-flowing water, so I ferried them piggy-back style across the deeper parts, and soon became saturated myself, stumbling on unstable rocks underwater.

Sketching while out with the family is something of a compromise, especially when everyone is wet, cold and hungry. Speed in executing the sketch is essential to stem the threat of a rebellion! Under these circumstances I rarely do watercolour sketches. In any case, fast-flowing rivers in spate are not the ideal places to get out a box of paints – if any fall in the water they are usually gone for ever. One sketch I carried out in the middle of the River Clydach worked well until I stepped off the boulder on which I had been perched, and knocked my rucksack into the water. Luckily, amidst peals of unsympathetic laughter, I managed to retrieve most of the soggy contents as they floated downstream.

◀ WATERFALL, GLAC NA GAINMHICH
This waterfall tumbles into a huge gorge in the Northern Highlands of *Scotland. The figure gives an idea of the size of the fall.*

▲ CASCASDA DELLE PILE, NORTHERN ITALY

▲ Morning
Sunlight, Chee
Dale, Derbyshire
240 × 340 mm
(9½ × 13½ in)

TYROLEAN TRAVERSING

We came to a place where the water was deeper and fast flowing, and so set up a Tyrolean traverse across the river. This involves a rope strung horizontally, across which we can pull ourselves. Unfortunately, the far bank lacked anything high up on which to fasten the rope, so I stood on a fallen tree-trunk, and with the rope tied to the trunk, passed it over my shoulders. The girls, all fairly light, came across one by one, hanging like fluorescent bats beneath the rope. Jo came first, and being concerned about her appearance, even in the river, took care not to spoil her make-up. She made quick work of the crossing. Caroline came across upside-down, her head just above the torrent – her anorak hood fell into the water, filled up and threatened to drag her away, but she made it across with a rather damp neck, to everyone's merriment. Catherine followed in her usual abandoned style – in order to make it more of a challenge, she flailed her legs in all directions, getting a few of us wet in the process.

The Clydach Gorge has been despoiled over the centuries. It must be one of the most beautiful places in Wales to undergo such ignominy. Tram-roads and iron-works once littered the gorge, and now a major road and huge power lines run through the heart of it. The river itself is festooned with the detritus of modern industrialized society, and the poisonous fumes from heavy traffic are at times unbearable when close to the road. Even as I write, plans are afoot for more highway developments, further illustrating man's callous indifference to the beauty of nature.

NATURE AT ITS BEST

When snow lays deep and icicles like tusks hang in rows from the rocky walls, this gorge glows with unparalleled beauty. The brief impermanence of this veritable Palace of the Ice King means that it is rarely seen by humans. Rocks covered in a thin film of ice are not the easiest to negotiate in wellies, but the reward is well worthwhile, for all of man's litter is covered, and the scene briefly reverts to raw nature.

▲ CLYDACH GORGE
IN ICE
To reach this position we abseiled 20 metres (60 feet) down a steep bank and gazed incredulously at the five-metre icicles.

◀ *Tyrolean traverse in the Clydach Gorge, South Wales. The river is in spate and here Caroline is secured to the rope by a sling.*

ENHANCING A SCENE WITH MIST

Gorges are complicated places to render as a subject when the light is good, but in fog or mist they make first-class scenes to paint. Mist will lose unwanted background detail, so when the weather is bad I often head for a gorge or river. I strongly feel that as artists we often strive to see too much, when in most cases we should perhaps be doing the opposite. Gorges are usually fairly sheltered places and are generally peaceful, away from the crowds.

If, heaven forbid, the gorge is bathed in strong sunshine, then I feel drastic measures are required to counter the situation and a certain amount of artistic licence is appropriate. Inventing my own mist or shafts of diffusing light is one remedy, combined with a mixture of soft images, hard edges and strong contrasts. This technique works extremely well to highlight the effect of the centre of interest. In places the hard edges of solid rock are broken up by the softness of dangling ivy or vegetation. A soft monochrome background creates a sense of atmosphere.

As well as losing a lot of unnecessary detail, the introduction of a misty background enhances the suggestion of recession, at once creating a sense of depth to the painting. Background shapes of trees and rocks, for example, if rendered as fairly weak silhouettes, appear as though in mist when set against stronger foreground detail. Gorges therefore make excellent subjects in poor weather conditions, especially in mist.

◀ COED Y BRENIN, NORTH WALES
By half closing my eyes while drawing in the background I simplified it considerably.

▶ CLYDACH GORGE IN MIST
205 × 305 mm
(8½ × 12 in)

CAMELS, KASBAHS & CRUMBLING CRAGS

I returned to the desert and found within me an inner peace. These people lived real lives in a harsh existence, far removed from the insidious materialism and avarice of the high-tech world I had come from.

The shock of the sounds, smells and sights of Arabia so soon after leaving the lush green fields of Pembrokeshire, took me aback, revitalizing my senses in an all-embracing manner. The smells especially caught my imagination, for not since Daisy the cow during a coughing fit, had deposited two kilos of ripe cow dung in my wellie, had I experienced anything so pungent. The frenetic music in the bazaars, thumping out at a furious pace, captured the flavour of the East. Fiery Yemeni tribesmen came down out of the barren hills, their robes criss-crossed with bandoliers, their belts hung with jambiyas, huge curved daggers in bejewelled sheaths, and long rifles slung over their shoulders. Banditry was rife in the mountains. In the early sixties

South Arabia was a wild place and the medieval practice of sticking severed heads on the tops of poles still persisted in the Yemen. Deformed children sat begging, their limbs deliberately torn into grotesque shapes by their parents to foster sympathy. Yet, despite these barbaric inclinations, the Arab world fascinated me. I was hooked.

DESERT SANDS

A few years later I found myself stuck in the Nubian Desert in the Sudan when a locomotive broke down miles from

anywhere, but it was some time before I did any real desert foot-slogging. This was with Jenny in the Djebel Sahro region of Morocco, on the edge of the Sahara, in Berber country. The Berbers are a fiercely independent race, culturally and linguistically separate from the Arabs. They mainly inhabit the mountains, far removed from the Arab plains and cities. Long after the rest of Morocco had capitulated to French imperialism, the mountain tribes fought on. Though bombed, strafed and having their rivers and waterholes poisoned by the French, these natural rebels held out until the early 1930s.

◄ *The author sketching near Djebel Toubkal, Morocco.*

► SUDANESE VILLAGE
165 × 205 mm
(6½ × 8 in)

ROUGH TRACKS

Our battered Renault slowly bumped across the rough desert track, followed by its own dust cloud. The parched ground stretched into the far distance with mountains ringing the distant horizons. The town of Boumalne became a speck below the distant Middle Atlas, while the Djebel Sahro drew nearer. After about an hour we curved southwards towards a cluster of dwellings dominated by the ubiquitous minaret, and both hoped this was Tagdilt.

Would we find Lacen Agdil, the guide who Mohammed, our contact in Marrakesh, had told us to use? In a village of this size it should be no problem – or so we thought! Our approach was observed from some distance, and a young chap on a bicycle was waiting for us as we drew up.

Did he know Mr Agdil? Our French was not scintillating, but his was worse, and after much chatting and gesticulating we were getting nowhere. However, he indicated for us to follow him and took us to a large building in the centre of the village near the minaret. Here he led us through a maze of courtyards to a room where again we tried to converse, to no avail. Eventually, the lad, whose name was Daoud, produced some photographs of himself with trekkers, and an identity card stating that he was a mountain guide. At last all was clear. He obviously did not want us to meet Lacen Agdil, as he wanted the work for himself. One of his wives arrived with a pot of mint tea.

By now the light was beginning to fade. We decided it was pointless trying to locate the original guide. Daoud seemed a likeable

◀ Enjoying mint tea with Daoud.

▼ Daoud and his mule.

chap, so we agreed that he should be our guide. Then came the problem of discussing the planning of the trip, which at times proved frustrating, and at others hilarious. It became clear that Daoud had little idea about how to read a map. This problem was surmounted by a little guidance from me, and he seemed happy with our proposals. We would leave early next morning.

As we discussed the expedition, a large family gathering assembled in the room to watch proceedings. Daoud produced a torch which was pretty useless. He asked if I had one. So, producing my headtorch from the rucksack, I put it on my head. As they did not appear to have seen a headtorch before, this caused a lot of merriment. I then proceeded to give them a demonstration on caving, crawling around the room on all fours, and soon we were all falling about with laughter. Later, they brought in the evening meal of couscous, followed by more mint tea.

MULE-PACKING

Early morning found me shaving over an
ornamental copper bowl, with an audience
noting every stroke of the razor. A light
breakfast, and then we were away,
following the mule and Daoud out of
Tagdilt, heading south towards the
mountains. The mule, who had no name,
carried our tent, rucksacks, water and food,
and we decided to call him Mulé.

The low light cast ultramarine shadows
across the mountainsides. As the others
walked on ahead I snatched an occasional
sketch, eager to make use of the light before
the heat of the day burnt the vitality out of
every subject. Soon we left the main track
and followed a footpath across desert scrub,
passing an occasional building. Here and
there roamed herds of goats, each watched
over by young children.

The sound of tribal drumming could be
heard in the distance, which struck me as
strange. On cresting the ridge the drumming
became louder; not far ahead lay a cluster
of mud dwellings and traditional open-sided
Berber tents. One of the tents brimmed to
capacity with drumming females, gaudily
clad in colourful dresses and yashmaks. As
we approached they both ululated and
smiled in welcome. We had stumbled upon
a Berber wedding festival and, with typical
hospitality, they asked us to join in.

▶ TADMAMT VILLAGE,
ATLAS MOUNTAINS
225 × 180 mm
(9 × 7 in)
In the collection of Mr
and Mrs Don Dixson

WORKING IN THE HEAT

Working in hot climates with completely different scenery presents a new challenge. So many people seem to think that this demands a completely different box of paints, but in the main I simply use more of the warmer colours, or whatever is needed. In this scene I was keen to capture the effect of harsh sunlight on the desert, using the Berber tent as a focal point.

The heat grew more intense by the minute. A large crowd of Berber tribesmen gathered around, sunlight glinting on their curved daggers. The rich colours demanded to be painted in watercolour. Mid-morning in the desert is not the best time to paint, the only advantage being that there is little shadow movement at this time, and keeping washes wet is a headache if any intricate work is needed. Because of the heat, I use more water than usual and at times a little drop of glycerine, but this needs care. When I first tried it I put too much glycerine in the water and the sketch took two weeks to dry!

The feeling of sunlight is reinforced by strong contrasts between the shadows and sunlit areas, with very little detail on the latter. Colours tend towards the warm, with the coolness of the blue sky emphasizing the warmth of the ground. The brightest tone that the watercolourist has available is the virgin paper, so the highlights have been left as bare paper. The sun tends to bleach out the weaker detail, rather in the manner of an over-exposed photograph, and so to achieve this feeling of strong sunlight I find I have to restrain myself with the detail.

▲ RAPID SKETCH OF A CAMEL

◀ BERBER TENT
225 × 320 mm
(9 × 12½ in)
In the collection of
Ian Dixson

BERBER BREAKFAST

We followed the tribesmen into one of the buildings, where the only furnishings were carpets at each end and the customary low table. The three of us sat on one side, while over a dozen tribesmen in traditional clothes sat on the other side. Most of them sported long curved daggers, a symbol of their rebellious nature, and stared at their guests. I showed a few of my sketches, including one of Ali El Mamoun whom I had drawn in Boumalne, and was heartened when some of the tribesmen yelled in approval as they recognized him.

Breakfast was then brought in. Piled high on a communal bowl lay a great heap of what looked like frog spawn. Our dismay turned to horror when a revolting-looking gungy green liquid resembling used engine oil was poured over the frog spawn. Daoud dived into the pile with relish. All eyes turned towards Jenny and me. To refuse hospitality would be taken as an insult. I took the bull by the horns, and with a great flourish attacked the pile with a spoon. With sleight of hand and much gesticulating to cause a diversion, I managed to dislodge most of the contents of the spoon, and tasted a small sample of the fare. It tasted like rancid potting compost, but even so, was certainly not as bad as it looked.

Jenny followed suit, and we managed to consume very little while appearing to dig in heartily. I then made indications of being incredibly well feasted, although in truth I was getting quite hungry! Mint tea arrived. There it is always served in small glasses, accompanied by flamboyant flourishing of the ornamental silver teapots, and poured

accurately into the glasses from a height of about a metre. Usually the contents of the glass were poured back into the teapot, and the procedure repeated several times, until the pourer apparently became bored. Sugar was produced in large solid lumps which were hammered with a piece of rock until they were small enough. Unfortunately, being a conglomerate, little bits fell off the rock into the tea, while enormous chunks of sugar stuck out of the tea-glasses like icebergs, making the tea sickeningly sweet.

◄ ALI EL MAMOUN
Ali posed for me, while I sketched him twice – once so that he could have a version to keep, and once for myself. His smile was that of an old man – he was in his eighties – but his eyes were bright as an eagle's. After the French subdued the hill tribes, Ali and his friends were bound in chains by the Foreign Legion and taken to Algeria and Tunisia to work building roads for the colonialists. During the Second World War he fought with the French at the Battle of Monte Cassino in Italy, losing all his comrades, mainly to land mines. He alone of his unit returned to Morocco.

▲ *Jenny with Berber headdress.*

The Berbers are adept at recycling – of necessity perhaps, but many of their schemes are ingenious. The sugar bag then became a form of wedding certificate, and was presented to the groom! At least that is how we understood it. After the refreshments I sketched one of the tents. They were not too keen on me sketching the wedding tent, so I began a small watercolour with an audience of tribesmen gathered around.

DANCING IN THE DESERT
In the meantime Jenny had been invited to take part in the dancing festivities. When I found her she was bedecked with Berber headdress, and leaping about like some multi-coloured mountain goat. Her *coup de théâtre* over, we said farewell and continued towards the mountains.

Barren soil gave way to rock. The heat increased, but we kept moving to make up for lost time, until eventually we stopped for a lunch break, settling down in the shade of a massive boulder while Daoud produced the meal. We had stopped near a well and a number of curious young urchins observed our activities from a safe distance. Afterwards I gave them some of our food, but they were terrified of approaching me. Perhaps it was the hat!

We ate, dozed and sketched until the heat of the day subsided. By teatime we were on our way again. Evening found us sketching a cluster of buildings in the shadow of a huge dragon-shaped peak that reminded me of Tryfan in North Wales. What a change from normal backpacking this was; apart from erecting the tent, I had

little to do except paint in the evening light and write up my log. Being able to sketch when the light is at its best is important, something which is often denied me when there is an urgency to carry out practical tasks before darkness falls.

Our journey wound up valleys in the main, travelling at an easy pace. We were amazed at how many people dwelt in such barren terrain. Daoud soon got the hang of our routine, which at first had been strange to him – stopping frequently to sketch and make notes. Mulé, however, found it bewildering; at times going round in circles, and at others taking off at a cracking pace back down the way we had come, much to Daoud's consternation. Each lunchtime and overnight stop would be at a waterhole – there were no flowing rivers in these mountains for most of the year. Without a guide it would have been extremely difficult to locate these points.

▲ DAOUD COOKING
Daoud cooked on a large gas stove which he placed inside one of the mule's panniers, out of the breeze.

NARRATIVE PAINTING

This scene is really built around the figures, which not only provide the centre of interest, but because of the space around them, give a sense of loneliness within a scene of utter desolation. The subjects are Jenny, Daoud and his mule. As we crossed the barren terrain I would move rapidly ahead or to the side, to ambush them with pencil or camera. On one such occasion I sat waiting for them for ages, only to find that they had taken a different route!

Whenever figures are involved in a scene I find it essential to include them in the initial plan, for if they are put in as an afterthought it never works quite as well. Positioning and size are critical considerations; figures close to the edge of a painting can look as though they are just about to walk through the frame, or are looking at something outside the painting's limits.

Before an expedition I do a lot of planning on subject acquisition: the different types, likely opportunities and how to tackle them, apart from all the equipment and materials needed. Obviously many subjects are opportunistic, but planning helps me to get so much more out of a scene. Tactics such as discussing with a partner how he or she can keep people talking, or bargain with them while you sketch them, are best laid in advance. When they wanted to sketch the North American Indians, the Western artists would get a friend to talk to the Indian while the artist

stood behind him, the sketchpad held against the friend's back. The Berbers resisted any attempts to sketch their women. I did try memory-sketching the Berber ladies, but this was not really satisfactory. Working surreptitiously is the only answer.

People working or performing some activity within a painting add considerably more interest than if they are simply standing around. This then builds the painting up into a story into which drama can be added, or even humour, as in the sketch above.

▲ RAIN IN THE DESERT
I snatch views of interesting characters whenever the opportunity arises, as these can be later used in a painting.

◀ DJEBEL SAHRO
IMAGES
215 × 330 mm
(8½ × 13 in)
In the collection of
Miss Sue Dixson

COURSING ABOUT MADLY

After a long siesta following lunch one day, Jenny began to feel wretched. While she rested in the shade with Daoud, I spent the afternoon climbing Kouaouch, a 2,592 metres (8,500 feet) peak in the heat of the day. As I returned, they were ready to continue. Mulé at first refused to follow the intended route and Daoud had considerable trouble as the animal coursed about madly in all directions. Jenny seemed as disorientated as Mulé, and extremely weak, but at least I did not have to chase after her and grab her nose! She could hardly move forward at all, let alone climb a steep mountainside. Eventually, with coaxing, we managed to get everyone moving in the same direction. I carried Jenny's cameras and helped her along. Her pace improved a little. Daoud asked if she would like to ride on the mule, but she declined.

Slowly we gained height, the views opening out around us into a stunning ochre landscape bathed in late afternoon sunlight. As we crested the top of the pass a range of jagged peaks lay ahead of us, silhouetted dramatically against the lowering sun. Daoud had gone on ahead. I could make him out below us, heading for what must be a waterhole. As we descended near some crags we met two young Berber lads. They came down with us, and I suspected that Daoud had asked them to ensure that we found him. By the time we reached him he had unloaded the mule and set out the blankets. His stove purred away cheerfully. The site lay in a secluded valley near a waterhole with a lovely patch of green grass on which to camp.

CHOOSING AND SKETCHING CAMELS

The two lads were nomad children who were camping about 150 metres away. They had camels, so I asked if I could join them to sketch the beasts. They were happy for me to do this, but I was quickly approached by their leader, an angry-looking Berber wearing a flowing green djellabah, and a face that appeared to have been embalmed in vinegar. He did not want his camels sketched. After much argument with the two boys he turned to me and rubbed his fingers together, saying 'Falloose!', which I knew was Arabic for money, although for a while I ignored him and went on sketching. He quietened down and walked away snorting while the lads pointed out the more interesting parts of the camels' anatomy. These were beautiful beasts with soft coats, the most well-kept camels I had ever seen. I must admit I feel more at home on a camel than a horse. The rhythmic action of the camel induces a soporific effect, calming the nerves. But choose your camel with care: breadth of chest, strength of leg and a good propensity to belch indicate a healthy beast. Of all the children we met in Morocco these nomads were the best-mannered and well-dressed of all, which says a lot for the nomadic culture. No holey jeans here, as with the nomadic tribes at home!

▶ NOMADS, DJEBEL SAHRO, MOROCCO
305 × 455 mm
(12 × 18 in)
In the collection of Mr and Mrs Don Dixson

▼ DRIED-UP RIVER NEAR SKOURA, MOROCCO

Dusk arrived and I returned to share tea with the others, giving one of the lads some money for Old Vinegar-face. Jenny still felt delicate, so she did not join us for a delicious vegetable stew. During the night I had to get out of the tent, feeling ill. Moonlight shone through a thin veil of cloud. I climbed part-way up a hillside to some boulders and viewed the scene, in my mind painting the cool grey-blue skeins of the moody desert night that flooded the valley in an ethereal atmosphere. The nomad tent was clearly visible in the cool-tinted moonlight. This would have been a superb time to have climbed a peak, being so cool, yet with enough light.

PAINTING KASBAHS

Our days in the Djebel Sahro will stay with us forever: the scenery and people made it memorable. Afterwards we returned to the Dades Valley. This is the fabled 'kasbah road', littered with hundreds of red and ochre-coloured kasbahs – fortress-like dwellings that appear to have survived from the Middle Ages. They are not all that old, however – probably less than 100 years – and erode easily in bad weather, giving the appearance of being ancient. This weathered and decaying aspect is appealing to the artist, and is something I accentuate in a painting. As Hugh Stutfield said in El Maghreb in 1886, 'Dirt and decay are undoubtedly important articles in the picturesque – were they the sole ones Marrakesh would be the most picturesque city in the world.' The kasbahs look very Biblical, especially with donkeys and camels in the foreground.

The journey towards Ouarzazate, the regional administrative centre, crossed arid desert regions interspersed with green palm groves near the river Dades. Wherever we stopped we were quickly besieged by Berber children, demanding *stylos* and *bon-bons*. At one point, completely surrounded on all sides by desert, we paused to sketch, and soon noted a cloud of dust, about a mile distant. The dust gradually grew larger, and turned out to be two children racing towards us at full speed. Even in such out of the way places it seemed impossible to get away from beggars! While we sketched most locals stood watching, at times talking quietly amongst themselves, although on occasion, when interrupted frequently, we indicated in French that we were working, and this they usually respected. We soon learned not to display too many pencils at once, as this led to a clamour of requests for them. On one occasion Jenny gave a pencil to the only child in the place, and within minutes was surrounded by kids wanting pencils! Many locals had a grasp of several languages, but Welsh was guaranteed to floor them!

▶ KASBAH IN THE DADES VALLEY, MOROCCO
560 × 735 mm
(22 × 29 in)
These kasbahs exude a medieval stronghold appearance. Most of them are crumbling, which helps to convey an aesthetic appeal. Capturing the feeling of sunshine and the arid nature of the surrounding countryside was vital, and the figures help to add life and colour.

CRUMBLING LANDSCAPE

Deserts take many forms, not just those with the archetypal sand dunes. When we explored the Badlands of South Dakota the terrain seemed a cross between desert and mountain, although it looked more like desert scenery in view of its arid nature. Layered sedimentary rock carved into spires, twisting gullies and pinnacles crazily capped with harder sandstone boulders, which locally they call 'hoodoos', form the heart of this bewildering landscape, surrounded by grassland prairie. Sculpted by water, grit borne on the wind, ice and even by lightning, this is the most rapidly disintegrating landscape on earth. The peaks are continually crumbling, their contours constantly changing. The Indians called it 'Mako Sica' – the bad land.

▲ BADLANDS CRAGS, SOUTH DAKOTA
225 × 430 mm (9 × 17 in)
As I sketched this scene I could hear rocks crashing down in places, as the landscape continually eroded. The layered sedimentary rock shows up strongly in places.

The Pine Ridge Indian Reservation spills into the Badlands. Red Cloud, last of the great chiefs, lived at Pine Ridge in 1890, when Big Foot and his band of Minneconjous decided that they would be safer at Pine Ridge. Sitting Bull had just been killed while being arrested, and the situation had become dangerously fraught. As the Big Foot band made their way southwards through bitter December frost, they were intercepted by four troops of the US Seventh Cavalry. By nightfall they were taken to the cavalry encampment at Wounded Knee Creek, where they set up their tepees. In the morning troopers surrounded the tepees and the Indians were ordered to surrender their weapons. One young Indian upstart wielded his rifle in the air and appeared to fire it. At this point the cavalry then indiscriminately fired their carbines at the unarmed Indians. As they fled, four large Hotchkiss guns raked the encampment with explosive rounds, massacreing men, women and children, including the ailing Big Foot and many elderly Indians. Quickly the snow turned red with the blood of hundreds. Shortly afterwards a blizzard overtook the tragic scene. Bodies were turned into grotesque shapes. The once-proud Indian nation died on that day.

HUNTING BISON

Until the 1860s the Badlands, with the attendant prairie, teemed with bison, but a three-year drought caused them to abandon the area. Then the American hunters came, driving the herds west, their bullets decimating the bison population. Millions died in the name of sport.

◄ PRECARIOUS PINNACLES, SOUTH DAKOTA BADLANDS
240 × 165 mm (9½ × 6½ in)
Hoodoos, formed by the erosion of the surrounding softer claystone, stand perched precariously, ready to come crashing down at any moment.

Thankfully the Badlands are now a National Park, and bison have been reintroduced, as we found out to our consternation. We had left the wagon beside the road and wandered out onto the prairie to sketch a colony of prairie dogs near Sage Creek. If we moved too close the animals would dive into their burrows, while behind us others would pop up at a safe distance to keep an eye on us. We spent ages watching and sketching them through binoculars, as they seemed to pray, hug each other and take the odd nibble of grass, all the time aware of our presence. Sketching through binoculars is a slow, awkward process, but with patience it can yield good results. The prairie dogs would hold a pose for some time before moving. Suddenly I looked behind and saw the massive dark shape of a bull bison moving between us and the wagon. A 4B pencil was no substitute for a rifle in this situation! Luckily the animal took no notice of us, so we waited until he had ambled further to one side before we made an attempt to reach the wagon. For about ten minutes he could easily have caught us at any point, but closer to the wagon we felt brave enough to stop and sketch him.

NASTY BOULDERS

We travelled on into the midst of the decaying peaks and camped overnight. Recently, not far away, a two-hour landslide had occurred, with rocks the size of caravans crashing down. This made Jenny nervous in the extreme. We decided to walk into one of the more scenically exciting parts to explore the landscape at close

hand. At first things went well. We stuck to a track which wound through mud-baked canyons, across dried-up creeks and through long grass, keeping a sharp eye open for rattlesnakes. In the scorching heat we threaded past dragon-shaped pinnacles, beneath towering buttes and gazed in amazement at the crazy shapes of formations perched drunkenly on the cliffs above. At any moment we expected a Sioux ambush!

My suggestion to leave the track and take a close look at one or two of the gullies completely unnerved Jenny. Simply walking through this alien landscape gave her the

▲ SAGE-BRUSH PRAIRIE, WYOMING

▲ SHEEP MOUNTAIN,
SOUTH DAKOTA
BADLANDS

collywobbles. She followed at a discreet distance, as we approached one of the more interesting gullies. This sported the ubiquitous hoodoos – boulders ready to topple off at any moment. I wanted a closer look at the rocks, to improve my sketching viewpoint. In places we slid, grasping for a hold as the ground gave way. Even huge boulders were not reliable. We had to be ready to leap in any direction.

Just as I arrived in the optimum position, two vultures circled overhead. I yelled in astonishment, and instantly realized that was definitely not the thing to do. Jenny, in her state of extreme nervousness, virtually collapsed in trepidation at my yell, lost her balance, and fell over. Luckily she had not been standing on precarious ground. But the vultures were the last straw, and she shot off down the gully like a rocket. I yelled to her to hang on once she was on safe ground, then began sketching the amazing scenery. When sketching we are used to wildlife moving at untimely moments, but it was a new sensation half-expecting the actual landscape to move! When I caught up with Jenny she had calmed down, well away from those nasty boulders.

ICE–CLAD SUMMITS

*Sometimes it is the crags,
sometimes the atmosphere, but so often
it is the sudden arousal of excitement at
seeing the fluted snow-shapes fashioned
with the care of a master sculptor, that
brings forth the urge to paint
in so savage a realm.*

▲ Loch Avon,
Cairngorms
*At the top of this
rough watercolour
sketch the spots
caused by spindrift
before the wash froze
are clear.*

Crouching to shield my sketchbook from the elements, I began laying furious washes on the watercolour sketch. Behind me the arctic plateau of Scotland's Cairngorms massif lay cold and empty, swept by a continuous battering of stinging spindrift.

PAINTING WITH ICE

Within seconds the wash laid on the paper froze, but not quickly enough to prevent thousands of tiny spindrift spots from appearing in the dark blue. My watercolour pencil rattled across the paper catching the reticulations caused by the icing up. The brush froze, its bristles as hard as the ice axe by my side. Perched above Hell's Lum Crag, it was something of a Homeric struggle to finish the sketch of Loch Avon below. Each wash needed a new brush until there were no more; but the sketch was complete.

Watercolour painting is like mountaineering; there are times when you swing between elation and sheer terror. So far the route across the plateau had been a doddle, certainly not preparing me for what was in store later. I now headed for Shelter Crag where I aimed to sketch Pinnacle Gully. My route contoured around to the right, then dropped down steeply through drifts of virgin snow. Thankfully the slope sheltered me from the wind and spindrift that penetrated everything. The ground steepened alarmingly. In lighting so flat any contours or shapes in the snow became impossible to define. A terrifying white void, of unknown depth, fell away below me, as though the rest of the world had been erased like a pencil mark. It was almost sheer, but whether four metres or forty metres, could only be guessed. At least there were no rocks down there, so I decided to go for it.

FALLING INTO A WHITE VOID

I stumbled forward like a blind man going down a steep embankment, unable to focus on anything, and expecting to crash down the slope at any moment. The snow gave way, plunging me downwards, spinning completely out of control. The breath was knocked out of me. I came to a stop as sudden as my fall had started, and lay near the bottom of the dip, unhurt.

Now began a climb up the far side of the depression. Through deep soft snow, it became purgatory. How far? I wondered. It seemed to take ages. By now the hours of daylight were fading away, and tiredness began to affect me. The light deteriorated, something which does not help morale when alone in remote places. Eventually I reached some rocks, and cheered up at their substance after acres of snowfields.

Cresting the ridge below a large crag, the ground fell steeply into Pinnacle Gully, with Forefinger Pinnacle soaring upwards, etched starkly against distant misty cliffs. It drew a gasp of excitement, and thankfully I began sketching the final subject of the day.

Of necessity, the sketch proved to be a rapid pencil drawing. Hard as I tried to visualize it, the scene appeared to be completely drained of colour, so a stark monochrome tonal sketch sufficed. Once

◀ FOREFINGER PINNACLE, CAIRNGORMS
330 × 225 mm
(13 × 9 in)

◄ SNOW AND ICE, YSGOLION DDUON 150 × 240 mm (6 × 9½ in)
Ice-glazed crags on the north face of Carnedd Dafydd and temperatures way below zero bring a chill of absolute inhospitability to this Snowdonian scene. Keeping up morale when sketching in these conditions calls for a flask of hot soup and several rousing choruses of 'Men of Harlech!'

finished, my sole aim was to get back to the car park, some six miles away. Descending back down the slope at a good pace, I soon found myself floundering in the deep snow at the bottom, trying to get back up the slope of my earlier tumble. Every step upward took enormous effort, and in such soft snow the ice axe was virtually useless. A number of false starts were made, trying to find the best route. Minutes ticked by and energy drained away. Pausing for some

chocolate, I then resumed the uphill battle. Progress at last. Slow, but deliberate progress. Suddenly the snow gave way. I crashed back down, and amidst flailing arms and legs, managed to arrest myself before I fell too far. Morale had soared, only, like my progress, to fall again to a new low.

Falling, even in soft snow, knocks you back and winds you. I gathered my breath and tried again, this time with more circumspection. Again, I made slow

progress upwards. By this time my mind was steadfastly locked into making sure I made no more mistakes, and I cast out all thoughts of beating the clock. Eventually I reached easier ground, with great relief. Not long afterwards my earlier sketching position overlooking Loch Avon appeared.

BLIND TERROR
Now came the final hurdle – crossing the plateau. Setting a compass bearing, I strode

out over the thin crust of hard snow. Visibility was poor, but did not present any threat, I thought.

Suddenly, without warning, the wind whipped up into a frenzy, bringing with it that dreadful spindrift, hissing across the frozen waste. To my dismay visibility dropped alarmingly. A snow flurry joined the spindrift, and within seconds it became a full-blown blizzard. Almost as soon as it had started the wind changed and, instead of hurling snow into my face, it came at me from behind. This was odd. Out came the compass, and with it the stark realization that within seconds of the storm starting I had actually turned through 180 degrees and was heading back southwards! So ferocious was the blizzard that my boots were not visible without bending down. This was serious. A whiteout completely disorientates. How long would it last? There was no shelter up here. Staying still would quickly induce hypothermia. Should I go on or turn back? Turning back would mean benightment. Should I try to make it to the Shelter Stone, which lay about two miles away, near Loch Avon? It would be hard to find in this blizzard, and was probably well covered in snow anyway.

I decided to continue on my course, heading for the northern rim of the plateau, in the hope that the blizzard would ease off before the precipices caught me. If I could not see my feet, what hope was there of spotting a cornice overhanging the cliffs? Tightening up my cagoule I resumed the steady plod, bent before the storm tearing into my face, clutching the compass in front of me, and following a bearing of zero

degrees. Surely this was the end – my chances of survival were minimal. Was my life supposed to flash before me? It didn't. My concentration lay in following the bearing and trying to assess distance. Thoughts of terror or panic were overcome by staring hard at the compass dial. Any fall in the ground ahead could herald potential disaster, but in a whiteout it is almost impossible to make out the slope of the terrain.

▲ LANGDALE PIKES, CUMBRIA
355 × 455 mm
(14 × 18 in)
Here the viewpoint looks down on the pikes from Bow Fell, through a window in the clouds.

For once I was not keen to hurry, but absolutely determined to fight my way out of this predicament. Suddenly a vague grey shape loomed ahead and to my right. I froze, trying to weigh it up. With extreme care I moved forward, realizing it was a rock – then another appeared. Now I could even see my feet! The blizzard must be slackening. Strangely the rocks seemed familiar – I had sketched them earlier in the day, right on the lip of the plateau! Momentarily I felt faint – a few more steps would have sent me over the edge. To say that my navigation had been spot on was to strongly discount my amazing good luck.

The blizzard faded away and the clouds lifted to reveal a distant Loch Morlich many miles away down in Glen More. What a relief! I walked along the edge, seeming to hang outside myself in a state of half-consciousness. Now that the effort was over, I had less life in me than a bag of turnips! Two climbers resting on a crag hailed me, dragging me out of my semi-comatose state. 'You look all in,' said one, offering me coffee from his flask. Gratefully I gulped down the warm, humanizing liquid, glad to see other human beings after the ordeal. We chatted for a while, and then I made my way down to the car park, still in a state of disbelief that I had actually survived.

MIND GAMES

The effect our minds have over physical capabilities never ceases to amaze me. So often when energy is needed to battle out of a thorny predicament, it is there to see you through the problem. The moment you are safe, the energy seems to drain away.

Another way in which these mind games function is the response to the surrounding scenery. One mile of walking in flat country tires me far more than two miles of steep, rough mountainside – it is all in the mind!

THE FANGS OF HELL

Sketching in the winter mountains at times means descending by an unplanned route late in the day. This happened once on Bidean nam Bian in Glencoe, Scotland, when glorious weather made me want to grasp every precious moment up high. As a consequence I had to short-circuit my return with a 200 metre (600 foot) descent down an extremely steep snow and ice slope. Two-thirds of the way down, the slope funnelled into a narrow gap, at which point black, evil-looking jagged rocks stuck out like giant saw-teeth. There would have been no escaping these monsters in any fall, and I had neither a helmet nor rope on me.

▲ *The author sketching on Beinn Alliginn, Torridon Mountains, Scotland.*

► COIRE MHIC FHEARCHAIR, TORRIDON MOUNTAINS, SCOTLAND
We explored this spectacular ice-rimmed corrie when force ten gusts threatened to spit us out of this savage amphitheatre like psychedelic turkeys catapulted out of the freezer.

◀ BLIZZARD BELOW
CRIB GOCH,
SNOWDONIA
225 × 380 mm
(9 × 15 in)
In the collection of
Catherine Bellamy

Tentatively I began the descent. The snow lay hard and both ice axes bit well into it. Ten minutes passed but still those infernal rocks seemed no closer. It gave me the jitters, just looking at them. My wrists ached. The light began to fade. Keep calm, I kept telling myself. 'You've survived so far – another fifteen minutes and you'll reach those rocks.' That thought suddenly made me wonder what lay below the rocks. From this angle it was too steep to see. What if it was an overhang? I might even have to climb all the way back up. The prospect momentarily paralyzed me. How fragile seemed the tissue-thin tenure of life; in a rare moment of common sense I resolved never to climb another mountain.

THROUGH THE JAWS

Gradually the fangs of Hell came closer. The last section steepened, causing more flutterings inside. Thankfully I grasped one of the rocks, but was well attuned to the fact that all was not yet over. I still had to pluck up the courage to look down and ascertain what lay beneath. Below, the slope continued at the same angle, until eventually it eased outwards in a gentle curve into the slopes of Coire nam Beith. I breathed a sigh of relief, though aware that it was still some way down, demanding nothing short of total concentration. There were a number of rocks scattered about, but at least they did not look as evil as the fangs I clung to. With dusk falling, I made my way down the final section with deliberation, both wrists now feeling the strain of the constant placement and removal of the axes. It seemed an eternity before reaching

▶GLYDER FACH AND
CASTELL Y GWYNT,
SNOWDONIA
330 × 495 mm
(13 × 19½ in)

safe ground, and a last look back up at the slope. Strangely, once safe, I hungered for another mountain; there is no cure once you are hooked!

BAPTISM OF ICE

Solo winter trips tend to be highly productive in terms of sketches, as there are fewer distractions. Having a companion normally means a more enjoyable day, even if the number of sketches is reduced. Although Jenny paints landscapes, the high peaks and rock scenery are not really her forte. Our first winter mountain trip together turned into something of an epic, as I misjudged her fitness.

On a dry but windy January morning we set off from Idwal Cottage in Snowdonia, aiming to climb Glyder Fach via Bristly Ridge. Snow lay deep over the mountains. Things went well as far as Llyn Bochlwyd, when we became exposed to severe gusts of wind which swept us off our feet amidst clouds of spindrift. I sketched the partly iced-up lake, its water etched dark and forbidding against the snow and ice.

A snow-shuffle slog took us up to Bwlch Tryfan, the pass below Bristly Ridge. Here a

► Spindrift and
Sunlight, Lochnagar
305 × 495 mm
(12 × 19½ in)
*I arrived in the corrie
accompanied by
strong gusts of wind
which tore masses of
stinging spindrift
across the scene,
completely blinding
me at times. Sunlight
glanced diagonally
across the forbidding
cliffs. A truly wild and
inhospitable place
in winter.*

▼ Bristly Ridge,
Snowdonia

gust of wind tore Jenny's balaclava off and sent it hurtling into Cwm Tryfan with the velocity of a cannonball. Behind a drystone wall we huddled together over lunch, well aware that Bristly Ridge was out of the question. Coated in thick ice and exposed to such ferocious winds, it would be lethal. I suggested that we go back, because of Jenny's inexperience, but she vigorously disagreed. She was determined to carry on, and seemed to revel in the excitement. I should have overruled her at this point, but foolishly decided to continue the climb. We would ascend some 200 metres (600 feet) up a steep snow slope in the lee of Bristly Ridge.

At first an easy slope led upwards. The quality of the snow was excellent. Higher up we began to enter the clouds. Tryfan became a blur behind us, and finally disappeared, yet the supreme wildness of

◀ NORTH RIDGE,
TRYFAN, NORTH
WALES
225 × 330 mm
(9 × 13 in)
*Tryfan is best climbed
when clouds are just
touching the summit,
an electrifying sight as
you gain height. So
much more of the
structure of the crags
is revealed than in
clear flat lighting,
when all the crags
merge into one
another. Here the
shimmering backlight
lends a luminosity
and air of mystery.*

our surroundings lent a dynamic beauty of rock, ice and spindrift. At times waves of blinding spindrift swept down the slope. We roped up, the exposure now more severe and the snow harder, with a 215 metre (700 feet) drop below us. With some difficulty I hauled myself up a vertical snow ramp in a rock band. Too short to find any grip, Jenny had to be hauled up the rope like a whale climbing a haystack, amidst much laughter.

We reached the rim, the summit now a mere 300 metre walk to our right. Already the light was starting to fade. The full force of the wind tore at us from the direction of the summit, bringing with it a horizontal battering of stinging ice-pins. Going for the summit would have been a crazy waste of time and energy. We began a fast walk eastwards towards the Miners' Track, my intended descent route.

After some time we reached a frozen lake, which I realized was Llyn Casegfraith. We had gone too far, so without pausing we doubled back and soon came to where the Miners' Track should be. Under several feet of snow it was not apparent!

OVER THE EDGE
In the dim light there was no time to search for the exact route. The ground fell away at

an easy angle towards the cliffs, so I decided this was to be the route, straight down into Cwm Tryfan.

At first all went well. Then we came to a vertical drop below a ledge. Through the murky gloom I could only make out white snow beneath us. No rocks – but how far was it down to safe ground? With 20 metres (65 feet) of rope, I hoped it was no more! I tied Jenny on. She was highly nervous. 'But I've never done this before!' she protested. I explained that whether she liked it or not, she had to go over the edge. There was no other way. I belayed myself against solid rock above the drop and waited for her to climb down. She could not do it. I sympathized with her. There was only one answer to the impasse. I grabbed her with one arm and, clinging to the rope, slung her over the edge like a sack of potatoes. Amidst yells and clawing at the snow-covered cliff, she disappeared into the gloomy void beneath my feet. Suddenly the weight came off the rope. She had landed in soft snow. Without waiting for her reactions I looped the rope over the rocks and lowered myself down, half using the ice axe, half clinging to the iced-up rope. Finally I tumbled down beside her in deep snow.

Pausing only to give Jenny a hug, I looked around to ascertain our position. Thankfully the ground sloped away gently, but below us lay a band of dark steep rocks that would be an obvious hazard in the dark. Coiling up the rope I urged her forward, not wanting to rest until we had put those sinister-looking rocks behind us. The deep snow clawed at us, but at least we had gravity on our side. By now it had become dark, though the whiteness of the snow helped us to make out any dangers. Stumbling towards the rocks, I led some distance ahead of Jenny to break trail for her and also to try to maintain momentum. At the top of the rock band I worked out the safest route down. Once down I felt easier. We paused for a brief rest so that she could have the last hot liquid from the flask.

Into the dark night we set course, Jenny finding it difficult to restart. I stuck closer to her, well aware that she needed to be kept going. Sitting down and letting a peaceful sleep come over you is extremely tempting in such conditions, but suicidal. Ages later we reached the road near Llyn Ogwen. Soaking in the bath that night was pure bliss!

▲ Eskdale Needle, Lake District
305 × 225 mm
(12 × 9 in)

PAINTING A PANORAMA

Painting a panorama makes a pleasant change from the usual format. Although there is a considerable amount of detail in this painting, I have tried to accentuate the right-hand summit of Mullach an Rathain. As it was much closer than the higher summit of Spidean A'Choire Leith, it appears so much more prominent. Here it is viewed from Beinn Alliginn. Carefully planned positioning of shadows and sunlight enhanced many of the features, something I studied for some time as the clouds created constantly changing tonal patterns.

For sketching panoramas I prefer to use a bound sketchbook, so that it is easier to work across the double pages, as in the watercolour sketch of the main range of the Brenta Dolomites. Sometimes I have to carry on over to the next page, which makes life complicated! Overlapping photographs is a splendid way of backing up the sketch. I rarely use a wide-angle lens on the camera for this, as it causes distortion and flattens the mountains. With such a wide expanse of foreground area, I generally abstract or vignette these awkward areas in the painting. The most usual problem that I encounter is getting home and finding that I could have done with a little more detail on one of the sides.

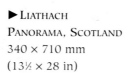

▲ BRENTA RANGE,
ITALIAN DOLOMITES

► LIATHACH
PANORAMA, SCOTLAND
340 × 710 mm
(13½ × 28 in)

PAINTING THE DOLOMITE SPIRES

For the artist, some of the most shapely mountains in the world lie within the Dolomites region of northern Italy. Spectacular peaks soar into the sky with unrivalled beauty and drama, the light-coloured limestone reflecting strong sunlight in an amazing variety of warm colours. In minutes violent storms can transpose these friendly looking mountains into the most horrifying and threatening scenery, creating an atmosphere fit for a holocaust. Painting in the Dolomites has taught me so much about colour, light, mood and drama, forcing me to reappraise my painting of the British mountains.

Each of my visits to the Dolomites have been slightly out of season, when there is more snow and few people around. One of the most spectacular groups is the Brenta Range, which Jenny and I climbed from the alpine village of Molveno, where I had been running a painting course the previous week. As our first day involved a climb of about 1,200 metres (4,000 feet) and many sketches, I had carried some of Jenny's gear up a few days before, and cached it in a snow crevice beside a massive boulder.

WATERCOLOUR AND MUESLI SKETCH
Early cloud gave way to sunshine, revealing massive plunging rock faces and shapely pinnacles. Vivid blue gentians were sprinkled here and there, looking out of place in such a wild environment.

A wide ledge led around the northern side and head of the Valle delle Seghe, with spectacular drops to our left. At one place a

tunnel had been cut through the rock to afford safe passage.

Then came the climb up to the Rifugio di Selvata, a hut standing in a sylvan corrie. Here we sat down for a picnic lunch, taking the opportunity to sketch all the time. Steep zig-zags led us to open, wild mountain slopes and the snow line. Nearing the Tosa hut, I dug Jenny's camping gear from the snow crevice and we settled in for the night, which was to be an intensely cold one.

▲ PUNTA MEZZENA,
ITALIAN DOLOMITES
255 × 355 mm
(10 × 14 in)

Sunrise brought a flash of crimson and gold across the sky above a sea of cloud, with many peaks piercing it like islands, awakening within me a desire to sketch even in my semi-conscious state. Hot tea soon brought us back to life. I strove to capture the scene before the full flush of dawn had receded into a series of greys, muesli accidentally contributing to the mess on the paper. Stowing our overnight equipment, we then set off with smaller packs along the Sentiero Osvaldo Orsi, an exhilarating route running parallel with the main Brenta ridge before winding round and passing through the Bocca del Tuckett to the eastern side. A good path led round the first rock buttress and as we congratulated ourselves on excellent progress we found our path blocked by a massive snow gendarme.

Although not high, it was steep. Below, the ground fell away almost vertically into a gully. No place to fall, I thought, banging the ice axe into solid snow. Steps had to be cut, as we had not brought crampons along. Once on the top, the drop on the far side was negotiated with a flying leap on to fairly flat ground.

Now the scenery really opened out, with the spectacular pinnacle of the Campanile Basso abutting the savagely serrated Gothic spires of the Sfulmini Ridge, taking our breath away. Here we lingered, sketching and admiring the stunning Dolomitic architecture, with its vivid orange, pink and ochre splashes.

An easy path led up and down, through a boulder field, and then over steep snowfields, beneath magnificent peaks.

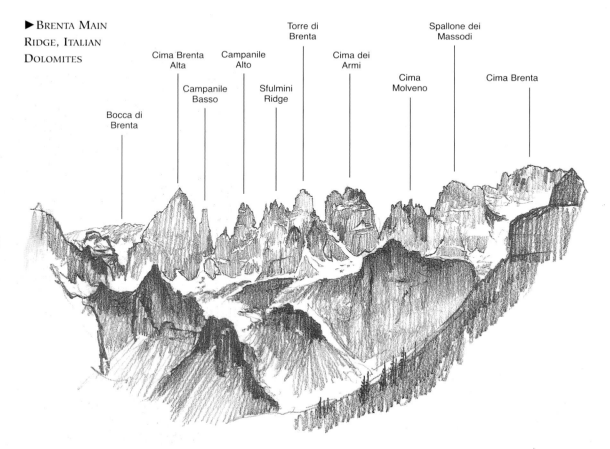

▶ BRENTA MAIN RIDGE, ITALIAN DOLOMITES

Although the snow lay firm these sections needed great care. One slip could accelerate us down the snow slopes, to shoot over the precipices onto rocks 300 metres (1,000 feet) below – a sobering thought. We completely lost track of time, soaking up the beauty and atmosphere. Clouds curled up from the valley below and wrapped themselves round peaks in amazing shapes.

Beyond Punta Mezzena we clipped ourselves on to the *via ferrata*, artificial metal aids in the form of cables, ladders and rungs set in the rock. These provide sensational airy ways of traversing the cliffs. With a climbing harness, two short lengths of rope and a karabiner at each end this method of progressing is rendered fairly safe. After a while, when we had gone just about as far as we intended, our route was blocked by massive snowfalls hanging over vertical cliffs that plunged down 300 metres (1,000 feet) or so. At this point we turned back, and returned to where we had left the overnight gear, having carried out several sketches of the amazing scenery.

At the end of the rope I used an axe belay to bring her up. Steadily we made upward progress in this way. Halfway up the mist descended. The height of the climb seemed deceptive, for it took ages to reach the col. Here we rested, hoping for a break in the mist.

On the far side, a snow slope led down steeply into the eerie mist, with rock walls on either side splaying outwards until they also disappeared. We continued. The mist began to lift and revealed more of the scenery. As I waited for Jenny, an Italian mountaineer caught us up and exchanged greetings. He had seen us earlier while we were sketching. Going on ahead about 100 metres (300 feet), he turned and gestured that he was on the correct route. I yelled our appreciation and indicated that we were going to climb up the cliff to do some sketching on the Bocchette *via ferrata*. At this he protested vehemently, indicating that it would be suicidal to go up there. Trying to explain at long range that we were only doing it to get some watercolour sketches seemed to confuse and aggravate things further. Again he pleaded with us to follow him, but I insisted on exploring the Bocchette. At this point he threw down his hat and stamped on it, then, waving his arms in the air, disappeared into the mist muttering to himself.

VIA FERRATA

Once we had recovered from our open-mouthed astonishment at this performance we made our way across to the cliff on the right where a splash of red paint indicated the start of the *via ferrata*. A little scrambling up good rock brought us to the foot of a metal ladder that led vertically up the cliff face. 'I'm not going up that,' said Jenny. 'OK – I'll just go up and a little way along,' I replied, and began climbing. At the top I stopped and took some photographs, suddenly aware of a presence beside me. She had changed her mind. Like me, at times her crazy zest for adventure overcomes her inhibitions.

Along the Bocchette the ledge ran horizontally, leading round the cliff past dizzy spires and buttresses. It eventually threads its way out on to the cliffs on the far side of the Brenta Ridge in truly spectacular fashion, but we could not do it this time, with too much snow and little time. After some sketching we retraced our steps and returned to the permanent snowfield. Over the next few hours we descended towards the Brentei hut through marvellous scenery, stopping frequently to sketch. The mist came and went all day, and apart from one cliff descent and a few steep snow slopes, one or two of which looked as though they were about to avalanche, all was easy going. At the Brentei hut we passed a small open chapel which had memorials to mountaineers killed over the years, each with a poignant photograph. Here we paused for tea and another sketch of the massive Cima Tosa, to the tune of thundering avalanches crashing down the far side of the valley.

▲ *Admiring the Campanile Basso, Italian Dolomites.*

BOCCHETTE ANTICS

The next part of our itinerary involved climbing up to the main pass, the Bocca di Brenta. This lay above the Pedrotti Hut, involving a steep snow climb. Jenny at this point seemed in remarkably good shape, though nervous about the steep angle of the route. Tying her on to the rope, I began the climb, kicking deep steps in the virgin snow.

▶ CIMA SELLA, ITALIAN DOLOMITES
305 × 380 mm
(12 × 15 in)

David Bellamy

EMPHASIZING MOOD AND DRAMA

Atmosphere and drama go hand in hand with a mountain scene, but sometimes when conditions are too benign these features have to be emphasized or even created. On this particular occasion both elements were present in abundance, the mist coming and going, entwining around the pinnacles and buttresses, and at times revealing what lay below or beyond. The drama and mystery of the Bochette route is incomparable.

Even when this drama and mood exists the artist needs to take care, as it is easy to lose. Careful positioning of the small figure not only adds a centre of interest, but accentuates the loneliness and perilous nature of her situation. Nothing destroys mood more quickly than a mixture of various colours, so all the colours need to be in harmony. In this picture the predominance of verticals lends a powerful expression of drama, further enhanced by the sharp pinnacles.

▶VIA DELLE BOCHETTE CENTRALE, ITALIAN DOLOMITES
305 × 455 mm
(12 × 18 in)

◀MISTY PINNACLES ABOVE MISURINA, NORTHERN ITALY
In translating this moody sketch of pinnacles into a painting, I would partly lose the edge of the furthest (highest) prominence with clouds, enhancing the air of mystery.

ARTIST IN THE UNDERWORLD

Perhaps, of all sports, caving, to the uninitiated, embodies all the hallmarks associated with deranged lunatics pursuing masochism to the ultimate. Combine this with the need to sketch from perilous positions, in total darkness, and you have a situation fraught with absurdity.

◀ *The author sketching in water.*

▶ THE BRIDGE,
BRIDGE CAVE, SOUTH
WALES
225 × 305 mm
(9 × 12 in)

Effortlessly I descended into the black void of Tunnel Cave, South Wales, an abseil of around 20 metres (70 feet). Most abseils work perfectly well and there was no reason to doubt that this one would not. About halfway down, where the shaft kinked, the ammunition box dangling beneath me hit a rock. To my dismay it burst open, spilling some of the contents before I could bang my right leg against the box, to jam it against the wall of the shaft. At the same instant my light went out. I hung in complete darkness, concerned about my camera in the box and that apparently the abseil ended on a ledge, below which was another alarming drop. Because of the kink in the shaft, the lads below could not see me.

Still holding the box against the side, I gripped the 'dead' end of the rope between my teeth and grasped the sack on my back.

Where was my spare torch? Had I left it behind? The important thing was not to panic. Then I found it – relief! I soon had light and was then able to rescue the ammo box without further loss. With that I resumed the descent to the mystified lads at the bottom of the pitch. The only things that had fallen out were a tripod, which was recovered intact, and a packet of crisps which had fallen on someone's head!

WHY DO IT?

Caving is uncomfortable, exhausting, painful, claustrophobic and often necessitates crawling through mud and negotiating short underwater sections. Slime Street, Greasy Pot and Worm Crawl are names of cave features that hint at some of

the delights of caving. So why do it? Personally, I enjoy the sensation of descending into the unknown, sketching the amazing formations and dramatic cave scenery, and also the photography, which can be much more demanding and creative than normal landscape work.

In caving, even a minor incident can potentially develop into a life-threatening situation, but considering the numbers that take part there are few fatalities. A sport which began with the use of ex-army and industrial gear, now uses modern equipment specifically made for caving, making it a lot safer. You can still lose your way, fall down a vertical shaft, be trapped by rockfall, get caught in underwater currents or rising floodwaters, but with proper equipment and know-how there is a far greater chance of survival.

►ENTRANCE PITCH,
PANT MAWR POT,
SOUTH WALES
330 × 225 mm
(13 × 9 in)
*The caver directing
operations at the
bottom is Phil Coles,
who is sometimes so
eager to get down a
hole in the ground
that he is said to have
gone caving in his
slippers! One caver,
climbing a ladder up
this pitch, apparently
lost his trousers
halfway up, causing
consternation to
those below.*

FIRST STEPS IN THE UNDERWORLD

My interest in caves began while walking
and sketching in Yorkshire. Nobody
interested in the magnificent limestone
region of that county can fail to be aware of
the many caves and potholes there. A
descent into Gaping Gill whetted my
appetite, and I explored a number of minor
caves such as Yordas Cave. Still, it was only
when I came across a book on cave
photography that my interest became
serious. The dramatic pictures caught my
imagination, and so I began to explore the
local underworld.

How would the family react to caving?
One winter's day while we walked on
Mynydd Llangatwg in South Wales, I
suggested we explore Eglwys Faen, a cave
with a large chamber by the entrance, once
used for chapel services when locals
became disenchanted with the Church of
England. Between the five of us we only had
three helmets and torches, so we could not
venture far. Beyond the large chamber the
roof lowered to a flat-out crawl through a
bedding plane. I crawled into the gap, about
22 centimetres (9 inches) high, followed by
Carrie and then Catherine, who did not
seem to mind that she did not have a torch.

It was foolish to go any further without
proper equipment. We returned to the cave
entrance. By this time it was pitch dark
outside, and Catherine, who was in the
lead, stopped to ask how much further it
was to the entrance, not realizing that she
was actually standing outside the cave! It
was two miles to reach the car, across rough
terrain. The girls had not experienced

◀ FORMATIONS IN
BRIDGE CAVE, SOUTH
WALES
150 × 255 mm
(6 × 10 in)

mountain walking in the dark before. 'I don't believe we're doing this,' complained Carrie incredulously, directing her fire at me. It proved to be a lovely evening walk, but the girls will never let me forget it.

SKETCHING IN THE DARK

As well as getting cold, some cavers become restless at hanging around during photographic sessions, so it is imperative that they are kept occupied. Many caving friends give invaluable support to our photographic efforts. At first these sessions were hopeless, but soon produced dramatic results, using flash guns to 'paint' scenes with light. Sketching with just a headtorch produces flat results, but with a powerful supplementary torch the lighting improves considerably. In a cave there is little to suggest scale, so increasingly I have included figure studies. This accentuates the drama of the cave paintings. Most of the time I use pencil or charcoal, although blobs of mud and even blood commonly adorn the sketches!

One day I called at Inside Out, a caving shop in Brynmawr, Gwent, and met Brent Durban who was to have quite an effect on our future caving exploits. One of his first questions was 'Do you dig?' This took me

slightly aback at first, until I realized that he was one of a band of stalwarts who not only caved, but dug to find new passages. Some spend years digging, following a slight draught in the rocks, perhaps getting only a few metres, or maybe making a breakthrough into a major cave system where no human has tread before. These days this is the only new wilderness left to find. Brent asked if we would like a trip into one of the spectacular local caves, Ogof Craig a Ffynnon, or Rock and Fountain Cave. I jumped at the chance, and one Sunday morning in April we entered the cave with three other lads from Brynmawr Caving Club.

Bill Gascoine, one of the leading lights of caving in South Wales, was leader on this trip. Bill had caved since childhood, and being a retired chemist with a specialism in hydrology, he is extremely knowledgeable about the streamways and geomorphology of the local caves. He had taken part in the initial exploration of Ogof Craig a Ffynnon. For a number of years cavers had been aware of the large amount of water emerging from a boulder pile on the north side of the Clydach Gorge, but efforts to dig an entrance were constantly thwarted by regular rearranging of the boulders by the amount of water. One big flood and they were back to square one!

▲ FORMATIONS,
OGOF CRAIG
A FFYNNON,
SOUTH WALES

STRAW CLOUDS

Then, in the summer drought of 1976, a hole above the boulder pile showed a draught, and local cavers John Parker and Jeff Hill enlarged it to discover a narrow passage.

Past the entrance we soon climbed into a chamber decorated with straw stalactites, each one so fragile that just to touch it would break it off. As they generally took many years to grow one millimetre, care was essential. The passageway grew larger and climbed up to a magnificent chamber, the roof completely covered in clouds of straws. It took our breath away.

On we went, into a narrow phreatic rift through which flowed an active streamway. In wet weather this part could flood rapidly to the roof. We arrived at the first boulder choke which had required explosives to rearrange the boulders sufficiently to create a vertical passage. At the bottom of a boulder choke you feel like a fly crawling through a coal-scuttle! Not only did the boulders look unstable, but water poured down on us as we climbed 8 metres (25 feet) into a large chamber. Beyond this the roof dropped, forcing us to crawl through the stream on hands and knees. This was the first of a series of delightful privations on a scale of 'dreadful' to 'sheer desperation'. The stream ended in a waist-deep pool with a low rock above, allowing little room.

After the pool the going became easier, following the stream past mud-banks on either side with fine formations, causing us to gasp when they were caught in the beam of our headtorches. A flat-out crawl up a flow-stone floor brought us to the bottom of a 14 metres (45 feet) vertical pitch. The first

part involved climbing a 2.5 metres (8 feet) ladder so dubious that Roy Morgan, an experienced caver, fell off it on one of our subsequent visits, taking my precious Nikon with him, to a deafening clatter. Amazingly he and the camera were OK, although the filter on the lens was smashed, and the rocks came off rather badly. I'm sure Roy is made of pre-Cambrian granite the way he flings himself about!

A fixed rope of doubtful quality led up to the most difficult obstacle – the second boulder choke. This zig-zagged upwards, vertically for much of the way for about 20 metres (70 feet), dripping, twisting, spattering mud and making me feel like a waterlogged towel that has been dropped in the mud and wrung out in violent twists. It took the first explorers seven months to dig and blast their way through this choke, working twice a week, with only a draught providing any hope. What the effort eventually revealed was breathtaking.

Out of the choke we dropped down into a large passage, which ran into deep mud. As the roof lowered, we crawled through parallel channels gouged by the passage of countless knees.

HALL OF THE MOUNTAIN KINGS

A tight crawl broke into an enormous passage. Travertine dams, formed out of calcite – the crystallization round puddles – held back shallow pools. Larger formations decorated the sides of the passage, glistening like lop-sided chandeliers. Eventually we arrived at the Hall of the Mountain Kings, a colossal chamber with 6 metre (20 feet) formations cascading over the break-out dome in the roof. This spectacular feature had stunned the original explorers with its sheer scale. Lighting it up effectively for photography proved impossible, but as the lights of the others played over the scene, I managed to build up a pencil sketch, gradually working in all the various features and adding in one of the cavers to suggest the immense size of the chamber.

I managed eleven sketches that day. Further visits unlocked more of the secrets of Craig a Ffynnon. Beyond the Hall of the Mountain Kings, a boulder choke so tight that our helmets had to bend to get through, led to a delightful 250 metres (800 feet) crawl. In places like this, mental attitude is critical. A nasty situation encountered miles from the entrance, with the realization that you could only be brought out in several pieces by a rescue team, can put you off for life! Beyond the crawl lay a long passage of comfortable walking. We continued as far as the fourth boulder choke, and then decided to turn back.

CAVE CONSERVATION

Thankfully, Craig a Ffynnon is gated, for if not the formations would never have survived. It is sad that in caves used to introduce people to the sport, most formations have been vandalized. Simply touching the stalactites permanently damages them. Conservation of these treasures is vital.

◀ *Gascoline Alley, Ogof Craig a Ffynnon, South Wales. Jenny is the focal point, illuminated by Catherine who is silhouetted on the left, and Dewi Durban from behind.*

▶ HALL OF THE MOUNTAIN KINGS, OGOF CRAIG A FFYNNON, SOUTH WALES
Here I have included a figure to suggest the immense size of this chamber.

LIGHTING UP FORMATIONS

Many wild caves contain formations that make show caves feeble by comparison. These works of nature's sculpture are like oversize still-life subjects. The artist has to arrange the lighting. Relying solely on a headtorch does not give the best effects, as the lighting is too frontal, so when time permits I set up my powerful Pelican torch in the optimum position, usually just to one side. This sturdy torch can take an amazing battering and floats in water – essential requirements in a caving environment.

In conjunction with the sketch I also use photography, bathing the subject in light from a number of strategically placed flash guns. The effect is truly spectacular and can produce dramatic results.

Planning is vital, as sometimes up to seven cavers are involved in the photograph. Each has a certain role, either as a subject or to fire a gun. The resulting photographs make valuable supplementary references to the sketch. Inclusion of the figure is vital, to give an idea of the size of the columns.

For the watercolourist, unable to lay light colours over dark, the straw stalactites are so thin that to paint the darkness around them effectively, is virtually impossible, so I had to resort to applying masking fluid with a fine nib where each straw was to appear. When this dried I painted the dark background area, and when the paint was dry I removed the rubbery dried masking agent with a finger. The oil painter happily has no problems of this nature.

▶Milking Parlour, Ogof Craig a Ffynnon, South Wales
165 × 280 mm (6½ × 11 in)

▲ *Brent Durban amongst stalactites. Here a flash gun has been fired by a caver beyond the furthest formations, with another firing over my shoulder. Brent is gently illuminated by reflected light. To sketch this scene I would return with one caver and a strong lamp, but the photograph is an excellent source of reference and useful in planning the subsequent sketching trip.*

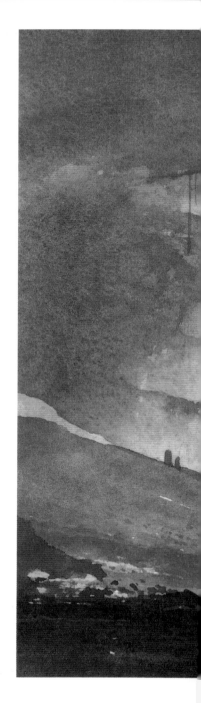

▶ KEYHOLE CHAMBER,
AGEN ALLWEDD,
POWYS
330 × 225 mm
(13 × 9 in)
*On the left, Roy
Morgan is traversing
the mud slope above
the horrific slit,
watched by Dewi
Durban. To obtain a
satisfactory view of
the scene I had to
balance on the edge
of the abyss,
sketching rapidly in
virtual darkness.*

cliff while on a walk, and wondered what
mysteries lay beyond this entrance to
another world. It contains a large colony of
bats, and although lacking in formations on
the scale of Craig a Ffynnon, it has much to
interest the underground artist. Five of us
tackled a route following Mainstream
Passage, an active streamway. At the second
boulder choke we climbed up and then
dropped down into the stream again, only
here we had to crawl through it, immersed
in cold water as the roof thrust down to
within centimetres of the water.

HORROR IN THE MUD
Once again, we climbed high above the
stream and into Keyhole Chamber, a large
passage, with a floor of dried mud. The
centre of the floor sloped alarmingly down
to an evil-looking slit, through which we
could see the stream in our torch beams, 15
metres (50 feet) or so below. The slit
wandered along the passage, a horror
constantly to beware of – 'A vadose trench,
is that,' said Bill Gascoine when I met him
later, his scientific brain reducing the horror
to less than romantic proportions.

At one point we had to cross the slit by
clinging to the side wall while negotiating
the top of a steep slope, above the slit. The
holds, slight bumps of dried mud, did not
inspire confidence!

Down a vertical crevice, we dropped
back into the stream. More passage led to
North-west Junction, now a long way inside
'Aggie'. By this time we all felt tired, but
determined to reach our objective, Cascade
Inlet. This we soon did, and marvelled at
the petrified cascade of calcite.

FURTHER LABYRINTHS
Ogof Craig a Ffynnon lies under Mynydd
Llangatwg, which also contains two other
cave systems, Agen Allwedd and Daren
Cilau. One day the diggers expect to link all
three caves into a massive system, which

would make a major expedition involving
overnight camps, so the mountain still has
many secrets to yield.

Agen Allwedd is an enormous labyrinth
of passages, over 28 kilometres (17 miles)
long. I had passed the locked door in the

Brent climbed up the side of the cascade and stood high up in an arch while I sketched the scene. Without him the picture would have been meaningless – no sense of scale, and poor lighting. By shining his torch in various directions he lit up different rock structures and held the beam where it best suited my composition. This co-operation between caver and artist is essential to get the optimum benefit. In one cave Brent stood for ten minutes under a waterfall, 9 metres (30 feet) up a ladder while I carried out a sketch!

Once we were rested the return journey began. By the time we reached the car Jenny was virtually in a state of collapse. The 45-minute walk across the bare mountainside swept by icy gusts chilled us, and my numb fingers had no feeling until hot liquid thawed us out.

CAVING PHRASEOLOGY

Although on occasion I have caved alone so that more time can be spent sketching, the best times are those with a small group, when humour and banter helps to surmount some appalling situations. The subtle phraseology amongst cavers often demands explanation: 'There seems to have been a bit of rockfall since I was last here,' usually means that we have come the wrong way! 'This next bit's a little tight,' implies that you will need supernatural powers to get through!

OGOF FFYNNON DDU

One of my caving ambitions was to explore Ogof Ffynnon Ddu, the Cave of the Black Spring – one of the deepest caves in Britain,

◄CASCADE INLET, AGEN ALLWEDD
330 × 255 mm
(13 × 10 in)
Once again, Brent Durban risked life and limb to climb the cascade, to light up the upper chamber, to lend a sense of scale, and to be the focal point of the picture.

over 300 metres (1,000 feet) deep with passages at many levels. My opportunity came one damp Sunday when I was invited to join a trip led by Paul Medhurst, with three of his friends. OFD, as it is known, lies in the Swansea Valley. We began at the top entrance and intended coming out via the Cwmdwr entrance, a long trip through arduous passageways, ending with a very tight section. There would be little time for sketching, but the experience would prove to be memorable.

We moved along at a fast pace, first following a large passageway, then chimneying down to the narrower Salubrious Passage with its strange white mud. A fixed ladder led to an awkward descent into the main stream. This, the Rolls Royce of underground streams, has claimed lives over the years.

UNDERWATER POTHOLES

We climbed down two large waterfalls, which I sketched, albeit in haste, while the others clambered past, or rested. Simply opening the ammo box while crouching in a fast-flowing underground stream is dodgy. Extracting pencils and sketchpad has to be done in a methodical and deliberate way, to avoid dropping them, and not capsizing the box. Even the simplest movement in these circumstances can become a calamity. If at the same time your light battery fails, it becomes tragi-comic!

The stream varied from knee- to waist-deep. Here and there lay potholes of unknown depth, hidden beneath the fast-flowing water. There was no warning – suddenly the bed of the stream disappeared and we would plunge into a hole. The water often covered the top of our helmets, and with the heavy ammunition box slung round my neck this constant kamikaze-style ducking drew both laughter and trepidation. Many potholes had underwater ledges; places to avoid at all costs!

We swam across a deep pool and eventually came to the Marble Showers, where jet-black limestone walls were streaked with thin white veins while water cascaded from above. At times we

◄ENTRANCE TO SHAKESPEARE'S CAVE, SOUTH WALES
A scene that has the appearance of the entrance to the very jaws of Hell!

descended waterfalls with water crashing down from an upper series at the same time. In a flood this must be a riotous place. After what seemed many miles, we turned up a narrow side passage. This was the start of the climb out. The passage ended where a stream cascaded out of a rent, 9 metres (30 feet) up the rift. The others began chimneying up the smooth-scalloped, holdless walls in turn. When you are tired, miles underground, climbing a vertical rift with no holds, in wellingtons, and a stream crashing down on you, with a heavy ammunition box swinging wildly at every lunge, the absurdity of the situation is brought home.

I took the chance to do a rapid pencil sketch. In these limited opportunities I concentrate on certain images. The overall shapes are quickly drawn in and then I emphasize one or two aspects – in this case the way in which the water crashed down

over the rocks, and also making sure to insert one of the figures to give it a sense of drama. Making the caver appear to be straining was important.

JAMMED

The emphasis now was on climbing, which I found easier than the latter stages of the mainstream passage where my poor light had made life awkward. Even in acute tiredness I relished the exhilaration at the vertical drop beneath me in places. My lack of a proper lunch began to take effect. The thought of that nasty squeeze at the very end loomed larger in my anxieties. What if I was unable to get through it? I could not face returning back the way we had come. At long last we came to the final 60 metres (200 feet) crawl. Paul shot through like a rabbit, but my wider girth inhibited such tactics. The lowering roof forced my helmet down until my chin jammed against the floor. To get my helmet through I had to twist my head to one side. The stones underneath frustrated every forward push. Even an inch was too great an effort at the crux, and much exertion was dissipated in simply pushing stones backwards! With one arm in front, the other behind and my chest jammed, I felt trapped, and had to rest frequently. Gradually my body squeezed through. The relief was immense. The final climb up about 6 metres (18 feet) of concrete tube in such a tired state shattered me, but how refreshing was the gratifying drizzle outside.

In caving you are entirely reliant on your companions. If you are immobilized they are your lifeline. I have been lucky in having enthusiastic caving friends. With all the paraphernalia for picture-making, a lot more equipment is carried than the average caver. All this has to be threaded through constrictions, across plummeting rifts and through fast-flowing streams. Without help it would be immensely awkward to transfer the gear across many of these obstacles, and safely pass across myself. Having such friends is the most important blessing in the world of the caver.

◀ SHAFTS OF SUNLIGHT IN ALUM POT, YORKSHIRE
535 × 355 mm (21 × 14 in)
This is viewed from halfway down the 60 metre (200 feet) shaft, with the stream disappearing into the darkness; below stands a natural rock bridge.

CAPTURING THE ACTION

After hours of hard caving we reached this point, a dramatic climb up a rift under a waterfall. As the others climbed, I sketched, eager to capture the strained movement of the climbers. Because of the wetness I used an underwater sketchbook with a water-soluble pencil, and later transferred the image onto ordinary paper. The sweeping beams of headtorches created dynamic images, often desperate as climbers fought to stop slipping down the smooth-scalloped rock walls.

As in so many sketching situations, having sketchbook and pencil easily available for instant use is imperative. Time lost trying to extract materials means that sketching opportunities might be forfeited. In caves, however, equipment needs to be well protected, which usually makes it less accessible. It is unfair to keep holding up a party by carrying out numerous sketches – I ensure the best subjects are covered and rely on the group becoming held up every so often at a difficult section. Then I can quickly draw in the basic structure of the scene, later on filling in the tonal passages.

Working in an alien environment and not knowing what is round the corner ensures a thrill of anticipation, but poses complications in the planning of sketches. At times the optimum sketching position relies on being jammed across a rift with a bottomless Stygian chasm beneath. You dare not drop your pencil – or anything else! Often a better job of sketching is done on a return trip.

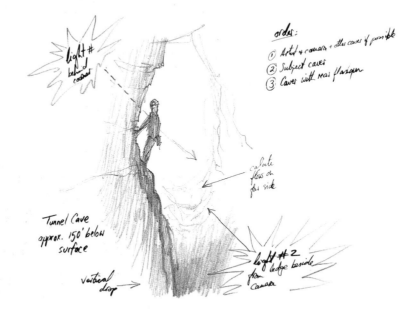

► PENCIL SKETCH OF WATERFALL CLIMB, OGOF FFYNNON DDU

▲ SKETCH PLANNING DIAGRAM FOR A LOCATION IN TUNNEL CAVE, SOUTH WALES

► WATERFALL, OGOF FFYNNON DDU, SOUTH WALES

WILD WATERS

Whether walking or sketching, I find rivers make fascinating companions. Being on them, or even involuntarily immersed in them, often adds that extra spice so necessary for a good picture.

In the wild places, rivers are a lifeline to survival. They can aid navigation, and be used as a transport system as well as provide water. They can also act as a barrier to be crossed. For the landscape artist they feature as an effective lead-in to the focal point of a painting, or even the main subject itself. In bad weather they make superb sketching subjects when other types of terrain become hopeless. Water means life, and to me the most exciting rivers are those that sparkle and tumble down mountainsides, their beds strewn with vari-coloured boulders. Not least of all, rivers and streams are sanctuaries for wildlife.

ACID RIVERS

In the English Lake District the Rivers Esk, Duddon and Great Langdale Beck are particularly attractive rivers for artist or photographer, the upper Esk flowing through arguably the wildest scenery in England.

Crystal-clear pools, reflecting the many hues of gaunt rock make attractive painting subjects, yet belie the fact that they are impoverished rivers. Sadly, acidification is affecting these water courses, and aquatic life is dying. Great Langdale Beck is virtually lifeless, with few fish remaining. There is a cost for keeping the countryside as we want it, and we must be prepared to pay that cost. In the meantime we desperately need to stop our rivers becoming streams of poison.

This sad state of affairs is equally true of the rivers in North Wales. One of the most picturesque rivers here is the Afon Lledr, which runs through a sylvan valley much painted by Victorian artists. Their compositions usually showed the river flowing placidly in the foreground, with figures or animals nearby. In the distance

would be a hint of wildness, usually in the form of the craggy peaks of Eryri, or Snowdonia. A walk along the bank soon yields these views, but for me a touch of white water in the foreground adds a powerful suggestion of movement and life, to contrast the solid rocks, crags and trees.

Nearby, the River Conwy, at one of its most picturesque stretches near the Padog Bends, is threatened by unnecessary road development. On every visit to the area I fear it will be the last time I see this glorious view, one of the most beautiful approaches to any of the British National Parks, so on one occasion I walked up the river itself to capture the scenes on paper. The Conwy can hardly be called a stream, and in places I found the water rather deep. However, I achieved some interesting, if wet, sketches.

REFLECTIONS IN THE WATER

Water is one of my favourite subjects – it adds sparkle, life and movement – but to paint it presents many pitfalls. Here the lovely reflections with the sparkle of moving water highlighting the more distant part stirred me into action. Mirror-like reflections may look good in a photograph, but to the artist they simply complicate matters. I prefer those with a slight blurring, enough to allow a certain latitude in depicting the features being reflected. In those cases you can get away with murder!

Simplicity is the key to painting reflections. I resort to using copious amounts of water in the washes, then dropping in the colours of the reflected objects and let the paint follow its course, delighting in the happy accidents that often happen. When this is nearly dry I then flick a damp, flat brush horizontally across the reflection. This creates a silver streak. Sadly, when many students try this technique for the first time and it works well, they get so enthusiastic that quickly the whole area is plastered with silver streaks, totally wrecking the effect, and giving the appearance of lateral railway lines in a paddy field!

Occasionally I come across a pool or puddle which could really do with a reflection, but there is nothing. I have been known to move a post, boat or other object in order to get my reflection, though I have not yet resorted to carrying my own post around with me for the purpose!

◀ CLOGHOGUE BROOK, WICKLOW MOUNTAINS
Brief, intermittent glimpses of reflections as seen in this pencil sketch usually excite me more than large expanses of mirror-smooth water. As I sat quietly sketching, a red squirrel came out of a bush and charged at me, turning away at the last moment.

▶ RIVER DOCHART, SCOTTISH HIGHLANDS
225 × 280 mm
(9 × 11 in)

snow-filled gorge late in the day. Below a waterfall which plunged into a sizeable pool of dark water, soft snow completely covered the wide gorge. I was camping, and it was vital to get across before darkness. Even so, I did a quick watercolour sketch before crossing. My heart beat fast as I took the first steps across the snow bridge, mindful of the strong current as the icy water surged underneath. Once into that deep water I would be a goner, with several tons of snow above me. Each step sank deeper, until I crashed through the lowest part of the crossing. The huge rucksack pinned me down. My legs did not appear to be in water, but extricating myself was like trying to get out of a giant bowl of custard with a sack of coal on your back. My ice axe flailed uselessly in the squelchy snow, and I sank further. Then I rolled slightly towards the far rock wall and, thrusting with my feet, grabbed at a sprig of heather sticking out of the side. From then on it was an easy climb up rocks to the top.

Sometimes a whole hour can be frittered away on crossing rivers or places like this, and it can be utterly exhausting.

▲ AFON NEDD FECHAN, SOUTH WALES
190 × 255 mm
(7½ × 10 in)

ICE-COVERED STREAMS

Immersion in cold water is fine if you are near the car or a hostelry, but in the remote mountains of Scotland it can be more of a problem. Hypothermia can advance quickly, so it is well to chose your moment. In winter crossing ice-covered streams presents a further hazard. Once, near Rannoch Moor in the Scottish Highlands I had to cross a

PAINTING WHITE WATER

Painting rivers in snow conditions needs care, otherwise everything can turn out too high key. This was effectively turned on its head one December day in Swaledale in the Yorkshire Dales, by the unusual colour of the water, when a light covering of snow tempted me out with a painting course I was running. Everyone was keen to sketch in the snow, despite the fact that this was not one of our 'action courses', which involve scrambling up rocks, walking and other energetic pursuits. We headed for Kisdon Force below Keld.

The route descends a rock wall in one place, but this was covered in snow and ice. Luckily Robert, one of our regular students, carried an ice axe – he usually has one on him, whatever time of year, 'just in case!' With great care we were able to get ten students down to water level. Here they had a magnificent view of the Swale roaring over Kisdon Force. The 'white' water, however, was mainly orange coloured, from peat moors above, contrasting beautifully with the stark whiteness of the pristine snow lying on the rocks and banks. Peat and soil erosion often turn river water brown or orange, but many artists shy away from making their water look anything other than blue.

RAFTING

The day Jenny and I went white-water rafting on the Snake River, in the Rocky Mountains of North America, it was flowing fast, a murky brown colour, swollen with June snow-melt. Sketching in such wildly tossing conditions with water crashing over you contributes immeasurably to the spontaneity of the work! By wrapping my left leg around a fixed rope I felt reasonably secure, but there is no telling when you might be projected into the water at high speed! In the rapids, when the raft hits a stopper – a depression followed by a huge

wave that crashes over you – it is tremendous fun, but it pays to have any sketching gear well secured for those moments when you are five parts of a fathom gone!

Naturally the results were rather basic, but afforded excellent material for subsequent watercolours. I always feel that we should refrain from allowing common sense to interfere with imaginative creativity.

▲ KISDON FORCE,
YORKSHIRE
320 × 455 mm
(12½ × 18 in)

SKETCHING IN WILD WATER

White-water rafting takes you into dramatic locations – scenery which demands to be sketched. The great advantage here is that the artist is in the middle of the river, normally an excellent viewpoint. Against this is the fact that the craft is bucking like an aquatic bronco, threatening to toss the occupants into the torrent, with huge splashes coming over the bows to wet the sketching paper. Here I took along an underwater camera as a back-up, but the sketches turned out to be far superior. In such conditions I use several water-soluble pencils and elasticate loose sheets of paper to a board, as I do not want to lose a whole sketchbook over the side.

It would be impossible to do a complete sketch if you waited for the optimum moment, when most aspects of the scene are at their best. My method is to start a little way ahead – I first blocked in the distant mountain scenery, then some of the middle-distance features, and finally as the craft hit the crux I rapidly put in the focal point which I had seen from some distance ahead, and had picked out as a possibility. This did not always work, but several sketches came out extremely well, and were usable once dried out! In the final painting I have altered the middle distance, basing that part on other sketches.

The amount of water coming over the bows (on which I sat) was at times overwhelming, and even washed some of the graphite off the paper, not to mention myself! I held my position with my left leg

wrapped round a retaining rope. At one stage we went through such terrifying rapids that the little guy next to me shot off the bows into the water. I managed to grab him and yank him back on board, but it rather spoilt the sketch!

◀ **SNAKE RIVER SKETCH**
This is one of the original water-soluble pencil sketches after it has completely dried out – note the tattered condition!

◀ **SNAKE RIVER SKETCH (ENHANCED)**
Here it shows how I have reinstated some of my original marks on the paper where these have washed off, and made the sketch more meaningful while still fresh in my mind.

◄WILD WATER,
SNAKE RIVER,
WYOMING
170 × 225 mm
(6¼ × 9 in)

▲ Railhead at Wadi
Halfa in 1966

Slow Boat up the Nile

A more placid excursion, sailing up the Nile
on a converted cattle barge in the 1960s,
provided interest at a less exacting pace.
Having been disgorged from a taxi at Aswan
with about seventeen Arabs, I found no sign
of river or boat, only a host of Arabs arguing
amongst themselves. I walked a little further
and came upon the Nile sparkling beneath
me. Moored against a rickety jetty was a
battered old bathtub of a boat. The whole
place bustled with chaotic activity as people
moved on and off the jetty. Everyone
seemed to be carrying vast quantities of pots,
pans, carpets, and all manner of goods.

Looking at the rundown state of the
converted cattle barge that was to be my
home for the next three days, I wondered if
this was really wise? Soon we were moving
out into the Nile, known at this point as
Lake Nasser. Along the shores, all that could
be seen were rocks and sand, apart from a
number of villages, all abandoned because
of the rising waters of Lake Nasser,
following the building of the Aswan High
Dam – a decision that did not endear the
authorities to the locals. Some houses lay
half-submerged in the water, giving the
appearance of a ghost town. Beyond lay
desert for hundreds of miles.

I took stock of my immediate situation.
Most of the deck was covered, apart from
the stern and a small portion of the forward
area where the crew operated. They were a
wild and excitable lot, prone to hurling
brooms and buckets of water at each other.
Above the boat a slender mast displayed a
rather tatty Egyptian flag; later it became
useful as a washing line. I descended the
wooden stairs into the hellish recesses of the
hold. As my eyes became accustomed to
the blackness, the sight took me aback.
Sprawled everywhere were Arabs in a
variety of dress, their belongings all over the
place. The only form of seating was a huge
pile of sacks. One rather dim light
illuminated the hold, and the air was hot
and stuffy.

Under Arabian Stars
The vivid luminosity of an Arabian sky after
the sun has fallen beneath the horizon,
heralded a starry night of intense darkness.
The boat was run aground on a sandy shore,

▲ River Nile near
Aswan
100 × 205 mm
(4 × 8 in)

and without the engines running an unearthly silence pervaded. Supper consisted of some foul-tasting Egyptian cheese between some equally foul-tasting Egyptian biscuits, being the only food I possessed besides three bars of chocolate and a bottle of cordial! I would need to be on basic rations over the next few days, until we reached Wadi Halfa.

After supper I slipped over the rails and onto the narrow ledge that ran around the boat. Moving astern, I clambered over the engine cover and hauled myself onto the roof. The boards were sturdy enough, provided I did not dance on them. Settling down in my sleeping bag beneath the stars, a feeling of contentment surged through me. The last place I wanted to sleep was in that gloomy rat-infested hold. During the nineteenth century the artist David Roberts had had a similar experience, the rats being so numerous that his boat had to be sunk to get rid of them! A bit drastic that, I thought!

I awoke shivering as the engines throbbed into life below. Bright colours blazed across the sky, though it took some time before the sun rose high enough to dispel the chilly air that hung over the river. As I arose we were reversing out into midstream, and soon began heading ponderously south once more. Nowhere on board offered any comfort. I kept changing position and searching the banks for any sign of life, in vain. The width of the Nile here was vast – several hundred metres. Large areas of water had the appearance of pea soup, caused by the submerging of all the greenery that formerly grew along the banks. The biscuits, cheese and chocolate were insufficient to stem my pangs of hunger. When we stopped in late afternoon I tried fishing to supplement my diet, but caught nothing. Very embarrassing when you have a large audience!

Abu Simbel

Around noon on the third day a most unusual sight greeted us – on the western bank cranes, trucks, men and machinery were spread out over a large area. Part of the cliff surface below them had been hacked away for what was to be the new site of the Abu Simbel temples. It was a huge task and as we passed I tried to imagine what the colossal figures would look like when reinstated in their eternal watch over the Nile. What a painting that would have made!

Cricket and Whisky

In mid-afternoon we suddenly turned sharply towards the western bank and drifted up to the beach. The Sudanese border was in sight, but we could not cross it until the following morning. Having stopped, I decided to make the most of it, and jumped into the Nile, enjoying a swim. The water was clear here. Then I spotted a piece of driftwood that made an excellent makeshift cricket bat, and with another round piece for a ball, proceeded to teach the Arabs how to play cricket. The 'ball' gradually diminished in size as each chip flew off, until it reached ridiculous proportions. The game whiled away the afternoon and was welcome exercise after the cramped conditions on board.

That evening one of the Arabs who often spoke to me said that one of his friends would like to see me below. I followed him downstairs where a number of men sat around drinking in the low light. We exchanged greetings and joined the circle. The elderly Arab sitting opposite me smiled, and to my astonishment produced a bottle of whisky. Their hospitality was overwhelming, for they would not let me drink just one glass. I must have put down several before leaving. We talked of many things, though the old man could not speak English, and my Arabic was minimal. Every so often we paused for a translation. They seemed intrigued by my venture alone through this part of Africa, which, in those days, was extremely rare. When I left for my roof-top perch half the inhabitants of the hold arose to say goodnight.

Even before I went below next morning we passed the large posts that defined the Egyptian-Sudanese border. The number of trees increased, and soon both banks were thickly covered. After an hour or so of false alarms we drifted in towards a small covered jetty. All order was lost in the obligatory panic: baggage appeared everywhere and the race to get off the jetty resembled the charge of dervishes at the Battle of Omdurman. Beyond the jetty stood a slight show of vegetation, before the hinterland became engulfed in sand once more. Low hills provided a background. The sun beat down mercilessly as we boarded a truck for the delights of Wadi Halfa, where a train would take me south towards Equatorial Africa, my destination.

▼ Deserted village
south of Abu Simbel

TANGO WITH A CROCODILE

In Africa the rivers and waterholes are the lifeblood of the wildlife. Once, while out sketching big game in Kenya, I decided to leave the vehicle and continue on foot alongside the Athi River in search of hippos. Foolishly, I tiptoed through the undergrowth several metres above the muddy river – the hippos would hardly have taken flight like startled rabbits, even had I brought a brass band with me! Nearby I caught sight of two turtles up a tree. Up a tree? This was too much like Alice in Wonderland for me!

There was no sign of anything in the river, until suddenly I was startled by a deep-throated grunt. The water rippled, and an enormous eye poked out from the murky water and glared at me. Was this a hippo? I asked myself. Better make sure. I photographed the strange-looking eye and then sketched it, hoping that further parts of this creature might emerge, both to identify it and enhance the sketch. But, alas, it took one more look at me and disappeared beneath the surface. So much for any great white hunter prowess – I had seen an eye!

I crept a little further along the bank, now high above the river and hoping for some action. It certainly came from an unexpected quarter – tiring of the river, and realizing that I was alone, with dusk falling, I swung round to go back to the safari wagon. With that, the ground beneath me erupted. In utter amazement I gazed open-mouthed as a mud-caked crocodile launched itself from under my feet, down the 6-metre bank and into the water with the speed of a bullet. Even below the surface its fast-moving bow-

wave was visible until it reached the far side. There had not been time to be frightened, but afterwards I was visibly shaken. Because of my stealth it had obviously not been aware of my presence until I turned. Had it spotted me first the consequences could have been alarmingly different.

Having always considered crocodiles as slow-moving creatures, this experience really stunned me. Needless to say, I returned to the vehicle with suitable circumspection, only to find that within a short distance a pride of lions lay in the long grass!

▲ ATHI RIVER, KENYA
180 × 270 mm
(7 × 10½ in)

SHADOWS IN THE TREES

Serried ranks of pines humour neither walker nor artist, but give me a broadleaved wood, or jungle, and ecstasy knows no bounds – I cannot fail to be happy there, even if I paint the most wretched impression of the scene before me!

Woodland, bush or jungle, whether close to a city or in far-flung places, can exude an enchanting atmosphere. It is often the most difficult sort of terrain in which to navigate, as one cannot normally see any great distance. This adds an air of mystique, as you never know what is round the corner. Passing a thick concentration of trees or undergrowth you can suddenly come upon a new vista or perhaps some wild animal, with unpredictable consequences. For the artist, pure woodland is complicated terrain, out of which a composition has to be drawn. Conversely, it often affords views of wildlife that would be difficult to obtain in more open country.

These places are often intermediate terrain passed through in order to reach the objective – a mountain peak, perhaps – although heavily vegetated areas can easily be objectives in themselves. Usually, though, I find massed trees and undergrowth need additional features to turn them into winning pictures. A stream, mountain, lake or animal fits the bill admirably. In hot weather massed conifers are airless heat traps, as I found out when walking through Wark Forest on the Pennine Way many years ago, in contrast to some of the African bush where the shade is welcome.

▲ VALLE D'OTEN, ITALIAN DOLOMITES
Much of the watercolour has been washed off by heavy rain, but in this sketch nature has captured nature far better than I could!

▶ ALPINE FOREST AND MEADOWS, MARMAROLE RANGE, NORTHERN ITALY
480 × 660 mm (19 × 26 in)

GETTING LOST IN THE TREES

Woodlands are special, mysterious places, that often foster a love–hate relationship with artists. Trees make superb subjects, but when seen en masse present diabolical problems of simplification. If there is no obvious path, stream or other focal point, then I usually home in on the most handsome tree and emphasize its beauty and structure. The others are reduced in number and suggested rather than put in with strong detail. A fair degree of mist or atmosphere helps, and invariably this needs accentuating or even inventing.

A technique I often use when in woods is to screw up my face, squint sternly through half-closed eyes, and cock my head to one side. Although this can be embarrassing, looking at the chiaroscuro effect of light seen through a framework of trees, bushes and saplings in this way assists me in seeing a composition. The monochrome sketch of woodlands in the Brecon Beacons is a fine example of this method. Sitting alone in woodlands doing studies of trees can be very therapeutic as I usually forget all the stresses of life and concentrate on the subject, occasionally interrupted by wildlife. Once, after three days of continuous snowfall in Austria I carried out many sketches in the forest, revelling in the snow shapes on the laden branches. However, when what seemed like a ton of powder snow crashed down on me as the tree swayed, it knocked both sketch and me for six. Luckily I was prepared for it and so did not lose any materials under the snow.

▶ MISTY WOODLAND
180 × 255 mm
(7 × 10 in)

▲ WOODS IN THE BRECON BEACONS, WALES

▶ WATERCOLOUR SKETCH OF SNOW SHAPES IN WOODLAND NEAR INNSBRUCK, AUSTRIA

SKETCHING MUD HUTS

One of my more unusual trips into bush landscape occurred many years ago in East Africa when I visited the Lost City of Gedi. The mysterious 'lost city' lies near the Kenyan coast, completely surrounded by bush. There seemed to be little information on the place, but a photograph of it had intrigued me.

In those days I explored East Africa by local bus, as this gave a fascinating perspective on the indigenous people and their communities. While waiting for a bus at Malindi I sketched some mud huts. A few days earlier the owner of another mud hut had emerged to ask if I was sketching her hut in order to build one back in England! Soon I was surrounded by chattering and jostling members of the Giriama tribe, all intent on seeing what this strange *mzungu*, or European, was up to. The huts disappeared behind the mass of villagers. To finish the sketch I had to leap up and down, which must have really given them cause to question my sanity. Then, in a cloud of dust the bus arrived, much to my relief.

Despite much revving up of the engine and banging on the side, the bus remained stationary for a long time. The ritual of increasing the revs to a deafening din, and further banging on the bus door every now and then, caused periodic frenetic bursts of activity, only to subside into another ten-minute delay until the driver saw fit to cause further amusement with another display. Eventually, with a full bus we set off along the dust track, and some time later I alighted at Gedi Village. The villagers were friendly,

but seemed puzzled to see me alone on foot – eccentric behaviour for a *mzungu*.

With the morning sun getting hotter by the minute I took a dirt track out of the village, and into the verdant bush, thankful for some shelter from the sizzling heat. It seemed a long way, but stopping to sketch I lost track of time.

THE LOST CITY OF GEDI

Eventually the entrance to the Lost City appeared, the jungle encroaching on its walls. It had been discovered and excavated by James Kirkman during the 1920s, in a state of ruin and totally overgrown by thick jungle. Founded in the late thirteenth century, Gedi was an Arab walled town with a palace, mosques, tombs and many houses. Mysteriously deserted during the seventeenth century, it became lost for many years. Some believe that the onslaught of the warlike Galla Tribe from Somalia might have caused the inhabitants to flee.

I stood alone, gazing at the ruins – eerie and mysterious in the surrounding jungle. Shadows moved in the trees. Almost immediately sticks and stones crashed down on me from the trees above, thrown by unseen hands. A large stone just missed me. I backed off, finding it difficult to see

anything in the masses of green foliage. My assailants eventually revealed themselves – a troop of mischievous monkeys! Fortunately they soon became bored with throwing, and I then explored the buildings.

The houses and walls were built of coral rag, red earth and coral lime, now mostly falling down in decay. Sunken courts with stone steps, dried-up wells, mosques and tombs, were all dominated by the great gateway to the palace. The powerful atmosphere of the place seemed to transport me to an earlier age, a feeling heightened by the isolation and the fact that I had only the sounds of the jungle for company.

The houses had been named after objects found in them during the excavation, or after drawings on the walls, as in the case of the House of the Dhow. The oldest was the House of the Cowries. At the height of Gedi's power cowrie shells were valuable and used as a currency.

Suddenly a shrill sibilating noise paralyzed my senses. At first I thought it came from the enormous baobab tree nearby, but whichever way I moved it became more intense and sinister. Any moment I expected a great serpent to descend upon me for daring to intrude on this incredible place. There seemed no

◀ LINE AND WASH SKETCH OF TYPICAL EAST AFRICAN BUS

escape from the all-enveloping noise, but then, after what seemed an eternity, it faded. I shall never forget that sound, for although I later found it common on the East African coast, especially during night excursions along tracks in the bush, the eerie atmosphere at Gedi had magnified its effect.

THE PILLAR TOMB

I sketched the tall pillar tomb with its backdrop of dense jungle. Pillar tombs are peculiar to East Africa, but there seems to be some doubt as to their significance. I found it difficult to concentrate and draw accurately. There were no crowds to distract me here, only flies and the occasional aerial attack, but I was also concerned that while sitting motionless a python might emerge from one of the many cracks or holes. Consequently I began to sing loudly and created a dreadful racket. The monkeys kept well clear during the choral interludes. Stiff with inactivity, I was pleased when the sketch was complete.

Nearby lay an enormous well, big enough to drop in a full-grown elephant, complete with howdah and accoutrements. A courtyard led into the Great Mosque where pillars stood in three columns; once these would have supported a roof held up by mangrove poles.

EVIL INTENTIONS

Beside the entrance to the west wing of the palace an earthenware pot had been buried, into which a djinn, or guardian spirit, was said to have been induced to reside. People of evil intent who entered would have been driven out of their minds by this spirit. Once

◀ PILLAR TOMB, LOST CITY OF GEDI, EAST AFRICA
215 × 180 mm
(8½ × 7 in)

more I began a sketch, trying to keep evil intentions to the minimum, standing beneath the vast baobab tree to do a watercolour of the palace main entrance. In those days I often supplemented the watercolour washes with ink line to strengthen detail, but the line tended to destroy any mood, and so I soon stopped the practice. Because of the amount of detail, the sketch took considerable time to complete, and soon the light began to fade.

This was no place to be after dark – visions of the ghosts of a thousand witchdoctors began to intrude into my imagination.

As I began the journey back, the warm air seemed charged with entrancing tropical atmosphere. The setting sun flung a vivid yellow glow across the sky, silhouetting the dhoum palms. Shadowy figures passed by in the gloom, each greeting me with the customary 'Jambo'. This place seemed to come alive at night.

I reached the village just as the local bus drew up, a customized bone-shaker of a truck. It was full to the gunnels, but that did not stop the driver urging me aboard. Well over forty of us crammed into the 28-seater. Then came a delay while a dismembered bed and other furniture were hoisted onto the roof rack. Bodies leapt up and down from the roof until sufficient speed had been attained to discourage these antics. We careered along at a cracking pace and soon reached the Mombasa-Malindi road where we came into competition with another bus. It became a race for each village stop, to the accompaniment of yells, thumping, and bits of furniture making a premature exit, as one vehicle passed the other. Why we raced escaped me, as our bus was full anyway, but I suppose it kept the driver amused. Eventually we lost the competitor when it came to unloading all the furniture at a small village, where most of the inhabitants seemed to have turned out to help. Arriving back in Malindi, African music drifted across the calm night air.

YELLOWSTONE MAGIC

Like the East African bush, many of the North American forests are teeming with wildlife. Yellowstone National Park in Wyoming is certainly one such place. The natural features of canyon, rivers, lakes and geysers, added to the abundant and very visible wildlife, make the park an outstanding visual experience. One of the early explorers of Yellowstone was mountain man Jim Bridger, well known for his tall tales. As one can imagine, when he returned east with stories of geysers, boiling springs, and pulling fish out of a river to drop it into a hot pool to boil it without taking it off the line, he was greeted with much scepticism!

Despite the drawback of large visitor numbers, the attractions were so exciting that I spent most of the time sketching in desperate haste. The geysers caught me by surprise, their dynamic contrast to rock and vegetation proving irresistible, yet notoriously difficult to capture in watercolour. By placing a pine tree against steaming, hissing geysers, evocative and atmospheric compositions simply yelled out to be painted. The colours of the rocks around the boiling waterscapes created a compelling spectacle.

◀ Bellamy at the Grand Canyon of Yellowstone.

▲ NORRIS GEYSER
BASIN, YELLOWSTONE

▲ *Sketching a bison,*
Firehole River,
Wyoming.

Sketching Wildlife

Yellowstone is a landscape alive with drama, excitement and beauty, and the visual hunt for its larger mammals – bison, bears, elk and moose – add a new dimension. The bison seemed tame enough, but could easily turn nasty without warning. Lining up viewpoints on the beasts was not easy. Photographs needed decent backgrounds, but when sketching the background was best worked in as a subsidiary consideration to the animal. It could even be done later. Although we could get close to the bison, concentration on sketching made us vulnerable to other animals approaching from behind.

Snow lay deep in places when we visited Yellowstone. In winter the animals keep warm by staying in or close to the hot springs, streams and geysers.

The Grand Tetons

Just south of Yellowstone lie the Grand Teton Mountains. Seen from across Jackson Lake this wall of granite peaks, one of the most shapely groups of mountains in the Rockies, left us spellbound. Grand Teton, the reigning peak, rises to 13,770 feet.

▲ Bison by the
Firehole River,
Wyoming
This rough
watercolour sketch
shows a placid bison,
but they can turn
nasty at the slightest
provocation.

Jenny did not feel up to climbing a peak, so we decided to climb up Paintbrush Canyon, over the top at Paintbrush Divide and down the far side, camping out a few nights. The canyon is named after the scarlet Indian paintbrush flower, abundant on its slopes. As we circumnavigated around the eastern shore of Jenny Lake, clouds obscured the high peaks, but gradually cleared to reveal an exciting panorama. Progress was punctuated by several sketches, and once round the far side of the lake we began climbing into the backwoods.

PAINTBRUSH CANYON

Opportunities for sketching anything other than trees grew limited. A good path snaked its way upwards, and apart from a few casual walkers on the lower slopes we were soon alone, keeping a sharp lookout for grizzly bears. The forest teemed with wildlife, at times making us feel that we were walking through a Disney film set. Hidden eyes watched our progress, and occasionally we spotted the watchers. A podgy marmot viewed us with suspicion from the safety of a crag. When we stopped to sketch him he decided to pose, holding his head aloof one minute, and giving us a fixed stare the next, as though demanding to know why we intruded on his patch.

In places gaps in the trees revealed breathtaking snow-clad peaks caught in the sunshine. We crossed the snow line and sketched sparkling streams cascading down the mountainside. Gradually the trees thinned, to be followed by large snowfields, climbing ever higher. The temperature

◀ MARMOT, PAINTBRUSH CANYON, USA
255 × 165 mm
(10 × 6½ in)
The wildlife in Paintbrush Canyon amazed us. Many species appeared quite near, watching our ponderous progress up the wooded slopes.

◀ Jenny in Paintbrush Canyon, Wyoming.

cooled and increasingly Jenny fell behind. The climb took its toll on her, but she insisted in continuing. Our target for the night's camp was Holly Lake, about 2,900 metres (9,500 feet) up.

As I passed a huge pile of rocks a little pika emerged from the ruck and began chatting to me in a high-pitched yelp. Pikas resemble small hares without tails, light grey in colour and friendly enough to approach to within 2 metres (6 feet). They cut up plants, lay them out to dry in the sun, and then store them underground for the winter.

Jenny caught up but was now completely drained of energy. We had to stop at the next waterhole. A steep slope lay ahead, and here I had ample time to gaze back and sketch the view of the canyon falling below us. Framed between the mountain crags on either side lay distant snowy peaks, pink flushed in the evening light. Our heavy packs now really made themselves felt. Above the steep snow slope the ground levelled out and led into a forest of lodgepole pines, thin enough from which to see the surrounding peaks. I moved with speed, zig-zagging across the deep hard-packed snow in search of a water source.

OUT OF CONTROL

I heard falling water before seeing it, and moved across to where it tumbled out of the snow to completely disappear some 2 metres (6 feet) later. We had to camp here. Soon the tent was up and a brew singing on the stove. Tea revived Jenny, but I wanted her to rest. Dinner came next, and as it cooked I busied myself with camping chores. Returning to the stove, I found it had gone out. Relighting it, I then went back to work, only to see Jenny turn off the stove. When this was repeated I suddenly realized that she was disorientated.

Staying close by the stove I kept an eye on her, and soon had her eating hot stew. She must be suffering from altitude sickness, I thought, exacerbated by the speed of our climb, and exhaustion. Directly after the meal I ushered her into a sleeping bag and brought her a hot drink. This improved her immensely. Then, just as she was beginning to feel comfortable I dragged her out of the tent: she simply could not miss the alpenglow setting fire to the crags above us. The sight enthralled us, for a vivid red glow hung across the cliffs, as though painted by some gargantuan brush. An unforgettable experience. She forgot her aches and grabbed her camera. What an end to the day.

BEAR ANTICS

Well, the day was not quite over. The food and rubbish had to be hoisted up into the trees away from the bears. Tying the rope to the ice-axe sling, I hurled the axe high into

a tree, aiming to loop it over a branch and down the other side. Unfortunately, the axe became stuck. I tugged on the rope. Nothing happened. Again I tugged with greater urgency. The rope crashed down, but inevitably the axe remained up in the tree. Cursing loudly, I decided to leave the axe there until morning, as I was so tired, and using a piece of wood managed to string the rope over the branch and haul up the food out of bears' reach. With that I gratefully sank into my sleeping bag, and slept soundly.

▲ TETON ALPENGLOW,
WYOMING
225 × 330 mm
(9 × 13 in)

The next morning dawned clear, apart from a few wisps of cloud caressing the crags above. We had not been visited by Bruin and the food remained intact. After breakfast I climbed the tree containing the ice axe. Alas, the branches of lodge-pole pines slope downwards, discouraging anything bigger than a spider from climbing. Additionally this one was liberally coated with a sticky resin which spread over my cap and into my hair as the cap slipped to one side. The high altitude badly affected my tree-climbing performance and it took ages. The only way I could climb was by chimneying between two trees. Some 6 metres (18 feet) up I managed to reach the axe and knock it down.

We struck camp and continued our upward progress, unsure how Jenny would react to the climb. A steep slope led upwards through hard-packed snow, but at this point she was hardly able to put one foot in front of another. Could she make Holly Lake, which must now be close? With a supreme effort she crested the rim above, and there in front of us lay the frozen lake with Paintbrush Divide rising steeply beyond. A magnificent sight. We rested in the warm sunshine, so strong that even when wearing dark glasses while sketching on white paper I felt pain in the eyes. Above us massive cornices decorated the divide, though they could be turned and the route forced. But Jenny had had enough. There was no way she would make it over the top, several hundred metres above. Sadly, we would have to retrace our steps.

◄ SHELL CANYON, BIG HORN MOUNTAINS
455 × 305 mm
(18 × 12 in)
Scale is suggested by the lodge-pole pines, and I wanted to give a sense of strong backlighting on the trees and granite outcrops.

◄ SOUTH BRUSH
CREEK, MEDICINE
BOW RANGE, USA
215 × 305 mm
(8½ × 12 in)

WILD IMAGES

We cannot always attain our goal, and this to a degree feeds the need for the unpredictable nature of adventure within ourselves. If the outcome of every trip was foreseeable, much of the appeal would be lost. A challenge with the cost of failure removed is no challenge. I have had my share of good luck over the years, but will continue to press that luck further, for nothing can enthral me like the fire and beauty of nature in its wildest moments. Being in the wilds engenders a strong feeling of respect for wildlife and the natural environment, and a sense of awe at how the natural jigsaw fits together. It is not necessarily the most shapely scenes that excite most, but those where light and atmosphere combine to create watercolours in the mind. These are the images that linger longest.

CAPTURING WILDLIFE

Although not really a wildlife artist, I do enjoy both sketching and being amongst wild animals when the opportunity arises. Timid animals are not easy to capture on paper and of course the fierce ones need careful watching, with an ability to react pretty quickly. A grizzly bear moves at about 30 miles per hour, which tends to put things into perspective.

The African buffalo is unpredictable and particularly dangerous when in a bad mood. When we came across this group I kept well out of range, and near the safari wagon, ready to run at the slightest hint of a charge. The backlighting gave a poor image and little detail, but the dark colour of these beasts makes it difficult to see any detail anyway. My main aim was to capture their attitude – one of curiosity and suspicion as they sniffed the air for our scent. Painting animals on their guard, suspicious or about to charge adds a great deal of tension to a work, though it is not recommended in real life!

►AFRICAN GIANTS
I sketched these elephants using watercolour and ink way back in 1977. As they were swaying about all the time I had to wait my moment to catch the right pose. Many mistakes are hidden amongst the loose pen work! I had two or three sketches going at the same time because the animals moved around, and was prepared to abandon the session at any moment!

►Buffalo in the
East African Bush
140 × 180 mm
(5½ × 7 in)

▼Red Deer, Glen
Licht, Scottish
Highlands

APPENDIX

This appendix gives those readers who wish to pursue some of the activities described in the text sufficient information at least to make a start. It is not an exhaustive list, but I hope it will point you in the right direction. Many of the activities are dangerous, and you are strongly advised to seek help via the organizations mentioned below if tackling something new. The bibliography on page 126 gives further information.

ART MATERIALS

I keep art materials and equipment for outdoor work as basic as possible, with the emphasis on accessibility for rapid use. In the time it takes to extract the right pencils from a voluminous bag, the subject might have disappeared, the light changed, or the angle altered to spoil the composition. I use a belt pouch containing pencils, an A5 sketchpad, and often a small selection of watercolours, three or four brushes, a palette and water container. The pencils vary from 2B to 4B, plus three grades of water-soluble ones, which are simply water-soluble graphite, and some black and grey watercolour pencils, which allow me to work into watercolour washes in rain or surf conditions. When more time is available, or a complicated scene confronts me, I employ a larger sketchbook kept in the back of my rucksack. All my sketchbooks are protected by strong transparent envelopes or a mapcase. When working on the coast I prefer a plastic paintbox, as the salt water would corrode a metal one. In canoes, kayaks, rafts, or anywhere that I am likely to fall in, an Ortlieb mapcase protects the sketchbooks further, although complete immersion will soak the paper. Water-soluble pencils are really the only sensible medium to use near water.

Caving is by far the most destructive activity as far as art materials are concerned. Until recently I used an ammunition box, which is robust, waterproof and large enough to carry photographic gear as well as a simple sketching kit. However, it has burst open so many times that I now use a Pelican case made of lightweight structural resin that is amazingly tough. I protect a large sketchbook, if I carry one, by keeping it in a drysack within a tackle bag.

I never carry an easel around out in the wilds, as a decent one is heavy, yet is still vulnerable to wind and snagging in trees, rocks, etc. At sea when swimming to reach a subject I tow the sketching materials in a drysack, double-wrapped for protection. Plastic BDH containers, available from outdoor gear shops, make excellent containers for really rough conditions in caves, canoes and the like, when you yourself might get battered. Pencils and brushes should not fly about loose, though. Put them inside a small container, such as a crochet needle case, or a tube sold in art shops. The finished paintings are completed in the studio, mainly carried out on Saunders Waterford watercolour paper.

EQUIPMENT AND CLOTHING

Caving and canoeing apart, a rucksack is essential for most of the other activities, whether a small day sack for short trips, or a huge backpacking one for several weeks. For overseas trips rucksacks which convert into suitcase format are available, should you wish to appear more civilized in foreign capitals. I use a Berghaus Scorpion sack for expeditions, as I know it will take a tremendous pounding.

Lightweight boots which give good ankle protection are fine for most of these pursuits, with heavy-duty ones for winter mountain work. We wear wellingtons in the main for caving, muddy estuaries and some of the gorge walks, often with wetsuit socks inside.

These days the popularity of fleece garments means that the outdoor activist and artist can enjoy working in bad weather in reasonable comfort. A waterproof anorak not only keeps out wind and rain, but, if large enough, can shelter sketching gear. I prefer a garment of Goretex, a breathable fabric, and my Berghaus Tartra has a pocket large enough to take a standard A5 sketchbook. Wetsuits, of course, are necessary for sea kayaking, wet coast traversing and deep immersion in underground water courses.

Apart from a first aid kit and spare food, we take a considerable variety of other equipment, depending on the activity, and you should take further specialist advice.

MAKING A START

For activities such as fell walking, mountaineering, climbing, caving, canoeing or simply rambling in the countryside, you can join groups or clubs, take courses at specialist outdoor centres, or perhaps make friends with those already doing the sport. The appropriate magazines contain addresses of suitable organizations. Coast traversing and gill climbing are activities that are sometimes covered by certain outdoor centres in the appropriate areas, such as Pembrokeshire in Wales and the Lake District in England. With caving it is highly recommended that you join a caving club, as you will then have access to club equipment such as ladders and SRT (Single Rope Technique) equipment, as well as colleagues well versed in the local caves.

USEFUL ADDRESSES

These organizations range from private enterprises, to conservation groups. Further addresses and information can be obtained from the relevant mountaineering and outdoor activities journals, available at most newsagents. Some specialized magazines, such as *Descent* for caving, can in the main only be found in outdoor gear shops, especially in the main British caving areas – Derbyshire, the Mendips, South Wales and Yorkshire.

Campaign for the Protection of Rural Wales
31 High Street, Welshpool, Powys, SY21 7JP

Council for the Protection of Rural England
Warwick House, 25 Buckingham Palace Road, London SW1W 0PP

Explore Worldwide Ltd
1 Frederick Street, Aldershot, Hampshire, GU11 1LQ
This is one of a number of companies who run expeditions to the Djebel Sahro region of Morocco, although I have not travelled with them.

Glen More Lodge
Aviemore, Speyside, Scotland
The lodge runs mountain courses all year round.

The John Muir Trust
The Membership Secretary, PO Box 117, Edinburgh EH7 4AD
The trust owns several mountain properties in Scotland.

The Marine Conservation Society
9 Gloucester Road, Ross-on-Wye, Herefordshire, HR9 5BU

Pelican Products
Sorrel Bank House, 25 Bolton Road, Salford M6 7HL
or 2255 Jefferson Street, Torrance, CA 90501, USA.
Pelican manufacture extremely robust lights and protective cases for use in demanding situations.

Plas y Brenin Mountain Sports Centre
Capel Curig, Gwynedd, North Wales
As the title suggests, Plas y Brenin caters for a variety of mountain sports.

The Sierra Club
730 Polk Street, San Francisco, CA 94109, USA.

Twr-y-Felin Outdoor Centre
St Davids, Pembrokeshire
Twr-y-Felin run courses and day sessions on various activities such as canoeing, climbing, coastal traversing, abseiling and windsurfing.

FILMS

Three videos featuring David Bellamy giving practical instruction in watercolours are available from APV Films, 6 Alexandra Square, Chipping Norton, Oxon, OX7 5HL. *Mountain Adventures in Watercolour* was filmed in the Lake District in summer and Snowdonia in winter; *Coastal Adventures in Watercolour* was filmed on the Pembrokeshire coast, and *Travelling Adventures in Watercolour* was filmed in Spain.

SELECTIVE BIBLIOGRAPHY

Butterfield, Irvine, *The High Mountains of Britain and Ireland*, Diadem Books, 1986

Davies, Cecil (translator), *VIA FERRATA, Scrambles in the Dolomites*, Cicerone Press, 1982

Dunn, J. C., *The Rocky Mountain States* (Smithsonian Guide to Historic America), Stewart, Tabori and Chang, New York, 1989

Evans, R. B., *Scrambles in the Lake District*, Cicerone Press, 1982 (includes gill climbing)

Judson, David, *Caving Practice and Equipment*, British Cave Research Association/Cordee, 1991

Langmuir, Eric, *Mountaincraft and Leadership*, Scottish Sports Council

Lavelle, Des, *Skellig Island Outpost of Europe*, O'Brien Press, Dublin, 1976

Price, Gillian, *Walking in the Dolomites*, Cicerone Press, 1991

Rowe, Ray (editor), *Canoeing Handbook*, British Canoe Union, 1981

Wright, C. J., *A guide to the Pembrokeshire Coast Path*, Constable, 1985

► FANTASTIC PINNACLES, WAPITI VALLEY, ROCKY MOUNTAINS
These red volcanic pinnacles rise high above the Shoshone River. To get a sense of scale, an adult would be about half the size of the small pinnacle in the bottom centre of the sketch.

INDEX

Page numbers in **bold** refer to illustrations